Future Mormon

D1523110

Future Mormon

ESSAYS IN MORMON THEOLOGY

Adam S. Miller

GREG KOFFORD BOOKS
SALT LAKE CITY, 2016

Greg Kofford Books
P.O. Box 1362
Draper, UT 84020
www.gregkofford.com

‒‒

Library of Congress Control Number: 2016935918

For Joshua and Nathan

Contents

Acknowledgements

Parts or earlier versions of some essays included in this book may also be found elsewhere. I gratefully acknowledge permission from the following sources to include them here:

"Burnt Offerings," in *A Dream, a Rock, and a Pillar of Fire: Reading 1 Nephi 1*, ed. Adam Miller and Joseph Spencer (Provo, Utah: Maxwell Institute, forthcoming).

"A General Theory of Grace," in *Exploring Mormon Thought: Grace*, ed. Sheila Taylor (Salt Lake City: Kofford Books, forthcoming).

"*The God Who Weeps*: Notes, Amens, and Disagreements," *Dialogue: A Journal of Mormon Thought* 47, no. 1 (Spring 2014).

"Jesus, Trauma, and Psychoanalytic Technique: Reading Bruce Fink's *Fundamentals of Psychoanalytic Technique* and Marcus Pound's *Theology, Psychoanalysis, Trauma*," *Journal of Cultural and Religious Theory* 9, no. 3 (Fall 2008).

"A Radical Mormon Materialism," *Element: A Journal of Mormon Philosophy and Theology*, forthcoming.

"Reading Signs or Repeating Symptoms," in *Christ and Antichrist: Reading Jacob 7*, ed. Adam Miller and Joseph Spencer (Provo, Utah: Maxwell Institute, forthcoming).

Introduction

A Future Tense Apologetics

These essays cover a lot of ground. They address a broad cross-section of topics in Mormon theology. But, despite their range, they clearly overlap not just in terms of their content—a handful of themes kaleidoscopically recur—but in their mode of address. These essays share a kind of para-academic tone that, while frequently borrowing from my professional work as a scholar and philosopher, repurposes that work for not quite scholarly ends. While substantially academic, the essays also tend to be both frankly personal and unapologetically faithful. They occupy, as a result, a curious middle ground. Not quite academic, they're not exactly meant for a popular audience either.

Who, then, is their audience? These essays are, I think, aimed at the future. They are aimed at my grandchildren. They practice what I would describe as a form of future tense apologetics. They mean to defend Mormonism, but not against the specifics of any past or present challenges to that faith. Rather than reacting to present tense criticisms, I see these essays as an attempt to proactively gather for future Mormons tools and resources that may be useful to them as they try, in the context of their world, to work out their own salvation.

I have three children, a girl and two boys. Our worlds overlap but, already, these worlds are not the same. Their worlds, the worlds that they will grow to fill, are already taking leave of mine. Their futures are already wedged into our present. This is both heartening and frightening. So much of our world deserves to be left. So much of it deserves to be scrapped and recycled. But, too, this scares me. I worry that a lot of what has mattered most to me in this world—Mormonism in particular—may be largely unintelligible to them in theirs. This problem isn't new, but it is perpetually urgent. Every generation must start again.

Every generation must work out their own salvation. Every generation must live its own lives and think its own thoughts and receive its own revelations. And, if Mormonism continues to matter, it will be because they, rather than leaving, were willing to be Mormon all over again. Like our grandparents, like our parents, and like us, they will have to rethink the whole tradition, from top to bottom, right from the beginning, and make it their own in order to embody Christ anew in this passing world. To the degree that we can help, our job is to model that work in love and then offer them the tools, the raw materials, and the room to do it themselves.

These essays are a modest contribution in this vein, a future tense apologetics meant for future Mormons. They model, I hope, a thoughtful and creative engagement with Mormon ideas while sketching, without obligation, possible directions for future thinking.

Chapter 1

A General Theory of Grace

We are, of course, saved by grace. "Trusting in the word of Christ with unshaken faith," we must rely "wholly upon the merits of him who is mighty to save" (2 Ne. 31:19). Or, as Moroni concludes, "if ye by the grace of God are perfect in Christ, and deny not his power, then are ye sanctified in Christ by the grace of God, through the shedding of the blood of Christ, which is the covenant of the Father unto the remission of your sins, that ye become holy, without spot" (Moro. 10:33).

In what follows, I will sketch a general theory of grace. As opposed to a special or limited theory, this general theory will treat grace not only in relation to atonement but, more broadly, in relation to the creation and the fall. Most debates about the role and reach of grace frame the argument in terms of sin and consider grace only in relation to atonement. But treating grace too narrowly distorts our understanding of grace, works, sin, and law. In a general theory of grace, grace names both a basic feature of reality and the defining characteristic of all God's work.

1. The Three Pillars of Eternity

In a 1981 Brigham Young University devotional, Bruce R. McConkie delivered an address entitled, "The Three Pillars of Eternity."[1] These three pillars, he claims, ought to structure our understanding of the gospel of Jesus Christ, and each of the pillars must be understood in relation to the others. "The three pillars of eternity, the three events, preeminent and transcendent above all others, are the creation, the fall,

---

1. Bruce R. McConkie, "The Three Pillars of Eternity," BYU Speeches, Feb. 17, 1918, available at https://speeches.byu.edu/talks/bruce-r-mcconkie_three-pillars-eternity/.

and the atonement. These three are the foundations upon which all things rest. Without any one of them all things would lose their purpose and meaning, and the plans and designs of Deity would come to naught."[2] More, "as the atonement grows out of the fall, so the fall grows out of the creation."[3] I believe that the same pattern applies when it comes to understanding grace. Grace as it is operative in the atonement can only be understood if one first understands its role in the fall, and grace as it is operative in the fall can only be understood if one first understands its expression in the creation.

We should begin, then, with creation. In the beginning there was grace. God's creative work is the most fundamental expression of his grace, of his willingness to freely give what cannot be earned or deserved. Furthermore, grace, rather than simply naming the *what* of creation, primarily names its *how*. Always and freely acting out of love, all of God's actions are acts of grace.

Grace is original. Grace is what comes first, and it is sin that then comes in response. Or, creation is what comes first, and it is the fall that then comes in response. Sin, at root, is a rejection of what God, by way of creation, has given as a grace. In Romans 1, Paul frames sin as a rejection of God's grace as that grace is plainly manifest in the glory of creation:

> For the wrath of God is revealed from heaven against all ungodliness and wickedness of those who by their wickedness suppress the truth. For what can be known about God is plain to them, because God has shown it to them. Ever since the creation of the world his eternal power and divine nature, invisible though they are, have been understood and seen through the things he has made. So they are without excuse; for though they knew God, they did not honour him as God or give thanks to him, but they became futile in their thinking, and their senseless minds were darkened. Claiming to be wise, they became fools; and they exchanged the glory of the immortal God for images resembling a mortal human being or birds or four-footed animals or reptiles. (Rom. 1:18–23)[4]

---

2. Ibid.

3. Ibid.

4. All biblical citations in this essay refer to the New Revised Standard Version (NRSV) of the text.

God's wrath, Paul says, is revealed against sinners. Sinners are "those who by their wickedness suppress the truth" (v. 18). What truth have sinners been "suppressing"? They have been suppressing the obvious truths about God's nature that, without any need for supernatural epiphanies, are already displayed in his work of creation. God's glory and grace shine in his willingness to freely give the whole of creation both to itself and to us.

However, rather than receiving this gift on its own terms, we balk. We flinch at its cost. We try to suppress it. We work to suppress God's glory by exchanging that grace for gods fashioned in our image. This is sin: sin is our active suppression of God's already given grace, as that grace is clearly (and even now) available in his ongoing work of creation. Or, in other words, we can't understand the fall without understanding creation because the fall *is* a sinful suppression of the grace offered through and displayed in creation.

Note, especially, how this approach reorders the relation of sin and grace. Rather than understanding God's grace as a secondary, mitigating response to our original sinfulness, our derivative sinfulness must now be understood as a failed response to God's original grace. Typically, debates about grace revolve around deciding the degree to which grace intervenes in response to sin, and, then, opinions differ about the proper ratio of grace to works. Some argue that salvation depends entirely on grace, some argue that salvation depends on some balance of grace and works, and some argue that salvation depends entirely on works. I would argue that, framed in this way, we've missed both the nature of sin and grace. Grace is primal and sin is a suppression of what has already been given. We don't have to work our way into grace; we have to stop working so hard to pretend we aren't already in it.

2. The Terror of Grace

Why would we suppress God's grace? Because it scares us. What God gives is beyond our control, much of it is difficult to receive, and a lot of it fails to line up with what we thought we wanted. More, because we're incapable of receiving, all at once, everything that God wants to give, God can only give a few things at a time. And because God can only give a few things at a time, all of God's giving also arrives as the passing away of what was previously given. That is, all of God's giving arrives as a kind of taking. Every new grace arrives as the loss of some part of the grace that preceded it. Given the brevity of our attention and the narrowness of our affections, God can continue to give only by continuing to take. Thus, every grace feels, upon arrival, like both an imposition and a loss. And, thus, we shrink from emptying the cup of God's grace.

Moses discovers this when God reveals to him the often suppressed truth about creation: the flipside of God's grace is our own nothingness. It's no wonder, then, that we duck and run.

> And now, behold, this one thing I show unto thee, Moses, my son, for thou art in the world, and now I show it unto thee. And it came to pass that Moses looked, and beheld the world upon which he was created; and Moses beheld the world and the ends thereof, and all the children of men which are, and which were created; of the same he greatly marveled and wondered. And the presence of God withdrew from Moses, that his glory was not upon Moses; and Moses was left unto himself. And as he was left unto himself, he fell unto the earth. And it came to pass that it was for the space of many hours before Moses did again receive his natural strength like unto man; and he said unto himself: Now, for this cause I know that man is nothing, which thing I never had supposed. (Moses 1:7–10)

We are reluctant to be the sons and daughters of God—"For behold," God tells Moses, "thou art in the similitude of mine Only Begotten; and mine Only Begotten is and shall be the Savior, *for he is full of grace and truth*" (Moses 1:6; emphasis mine)—because this revelation comes paired with the revelation of our own nothingness. It comes paired with a display of our own lack of control over the graces that have, do, and will come. This lack of control is both frustrating and frightening. So we suppress it. We set ourselves up, both personally and collectively, as lords of the earth and judges of what graces we will and won't receive. We cast ourselves as gods, as idols fashioned in the image of God, and the integrity of this idolatry depends on the strength of the illusions we can generate to either suppress the truth or distract ourselves from it.

But, in the end, there is nowhere to hide from God's grace. It gives itself relentlessly. It gives itself in life and it gives itself in death. It gives itself in what we want and in what we do not want. And the more we think we can earn and, thus, control, what is given, the more futile our idolatrous schemes will show themselves to be. King Benjamin, outlining this dynamic, describes faith as our willingness to trust, rather than dodge, the gift of our own nothingness:

> I say unto you, my brethren, that if you should render all the thanks and praise which your whole soul has power to possess, to that God who has created you, and has kept and preserved you, and has caused that ye should rejoice, and has granted that ye should live in peace one with another—I say unto you that if ye should serve him who has created you from the beginning, and is preserving you from day to day, by lending you breath, that ye may live and move and do according to your own will, and even supporting you from one moment to another—I say, if ye should serve him with all your whole souls yet ye would be unprofitable servants. And behold, all that he requires of you is to keep his commandments; and he has promised you that if ye would keep his commandments ye should prosper in the land; and he never doth vary from that which he hath said; therefore, if ye do keep his commandments he doth bless you and prosper you. And now, in the first place, he hath created you, and granted unto you your lives, for which ye are indebted unto him. And secondly, he doth require that ye should do as he hath commanded you; for which if ye do, he doth immediately bless you; and therefore he hath paid you. And ye are still indebted unto him, and are, and will be, forever and ever; therefore, of what have ye to boast? And now I ask, can ye say aught of yourselves? I answer you, Nay. Ye cannot say that ye are even as much as the dust of the earth; yet ye were created of the dust of the earth; but behold, it belongeth to him who created you. (Mosiah 2:20–25)

In the face of God's insistent grace, we can say aught of ourselves. We are less than the dust of the earth. And even this dust—even the dust that composes us—is given only as a temporary grace. We borrow earth to live and air to breathe and, in the end, we will have to return them both. Sin, though, *reads these gifts as debts* and, fearfully, tries to avoid them.

Potential strategies for avoiding grace span the whole of human behavior, but we should note, in particular, one surprising approach to sin: strict obedience. One strategy for suppressing the truth and avoiding God's grace is to put God in *your* debt. Here, the more obedient I become, the less I figure I'll be indebted to God, the less grace I'll need, and the more in control I'll become. Obedience, as a strategy for avoiding God's grace, is, of course, highly ironic. But religion, though it is meant to reconcile us to God's grace, always casts this distorted shadow. It always bears this alternate possibility for abuse. Religion, practiced as a way of indebting God to us—as a way of canceling God's grace and our own indebtedness—can be a powerful means of suppressing the truth. Religion may be, in some respects, sin's most successful strategy.

3. A Broken Law

As King Benjamin points out, obedience cannot save us from grace because obedience blesses us, and thus, exposes us more and more profoundly to grace. Our lives are a gift, the law is itself a gift, and fulfilling the law brings more gifts. None of it can be earned and none of it can be repaid. Obedience cannot balance the books. And, moreover, to the extent that we use obedience as a strategy for suppressing our dependence on God's grace, obedience itself becomes—ironically—a hallmark of our sinfulness.

Obedience depends on law. And to understand the role of the law in atonement we must understand that the law is meant to be an expression of and a vehicle for grace. Only grace can fulfill the law. We fulfill the law when we receive what is given as the grace that it is and, then, when we respond with grace in turn. In other words, the end of the law is love and only love can fulfill the law. Asked about which law is the greatest, Jesus replied: "'You shall love the Lord your God with all your heart, and with all your soul, and with all your mind.' This is the greatest and first commandment. And a second is like it: 'You shall love your neighbor as yourself.' On these two commandments hang all the law and the prophets" (Matt. 22:37–40).

The point of the law is love. And while obedience is generally better than disobedience, obedience in itself cannot fulfill the law. Only love can fulfill the law. However, love is a curious end for a law. Normally, the point of a law is to compel obedience, not love. As a result, making love the point of the law introduces a kind of knot—a kind of torsion or structural catch-22—into the heart of the law itself because love, if compelled, is no longer love. Love that is not freely given is not love. Love, as the end of the law, divides the law against itself. Love hamstrings the law in relation to its own assigned end because the law, working to compel obedience, cannot, in this instance, be fulfilled by way of obedience. It can, instead, only be fulfilled by a love that the law cannot—and must not—compel. The law must compromise its own integrity in order to achieve its assigned end. The law, compromised in this way, is broken. Not only is the law broken by our individual acts of disobedience but the law is, in general, broken by the grace that fulfills it. The law is too small, too weak a vessel to contain it.

This is a strange state of affairs. And it is this strange twist at the heart of the law that leaves the law open for abuse. It's this twist that leaves the law open to being hijacked by sin and repurposed as a tool for suppressing rather than enlivening grace. Obedience to the law, valorized on its own terms, becomes an obstacle to fulfilling the law's purpose in love. And the law itself, understood as what marks us as guilty and indebted, no longer shows up as an organ of grace. In Romans 7, Paul is quite clear about how this happens. Trying to untangle law from sin while clarifying the trouble that follows when the law itself gets hijacked by sin as a means for suppressing grace, Paul says:

> What then should we say? That the law is sin? By no means! Yet, if it had not been for the law, I would not have known sin. I would not have known what it is to covet if the law had not said, "You shall not covet." But sin, seizing an opportunity in the commandment, produced in me all kinds of covetousness. Apart from the law sin lies dead. I was once alive apart from the law, but when the commandment came, sin revived and I died, and the very commandment that promised life proved to be death to me. For sin, seizing an opportunity in the commandment, deceived me and through it killed me. So the law is holy, and the commandment is holy and just and good. Did what is good, then, bring death to me? By no means! It was sin, working death in me through what is good, in order that sin might be shown to be sin, and through the commandment might become sinful beyond measure. (Rom. 7:7–13)

Paul here describes an oblique process through which the law itself, good while yoked with grace as a vehicle for love, is instead hijacked by sin. Sin, he says, "seizes an opportunity in the commandment" to deceive us and cut us off from the source of life (v. 8). The law is supposed to connect us to love and grace, it is supposed to be holy and good. But sin repurposes the law—even obedience to the law—as a way of frustrating love. Sin, Paul says, is the thing "working death in me *through what is good*" (v. 13; emphasis mine).

4. Fulfilling the Law

We find ourselves, then, in a bind. Not only are we incapable of perfect obedience but perfect obedience, were it possible, still could not fulfill the law. The law cannot be fulfilled by way of obedience. It can only be fulfilled by a love that, unlike obedience, must be freely given and cannot be commanded or compelled. As Dieter F. Uchtdorf puts it, it is clear that "salvation cannot be bought with the currency of obedience."[5] What, then, is to be done? We must love. The law must be rescued from itself by way of love. And if we, ultimately, find ourselves capable of love, it will only be because God first loved us. "Love has been perfected among us in this: that we may have boldness on the day of judgment, because as he is, so are we in this world. There is no fear in love, but perfect love casts out fear; for fear has to do with punishment, and whoever fears has not reached perfection in love. We love because he first loved us" (1 Jn. 4:17–19). Perfect love casts out all fear. And fear, linked here with punishment, follows from a misunderstanding of the law. The law, because it punishes, is apt to provoke fear rather than love. But if we love, it's not because the law commanded us to love, it is because God loved us first. And, in light of love's revelation, even "punishments" can show up as gifts.

Now, God's love for us, his grace, is manifest first and most fundamentally in the work of creation. By creating us, he gives us life and gives us the world. But, too, God's grace is manifest not only in his work of creation but in his commitment to the work of *re*-creation. That is, God's grace is manifest in atonement. Atonement, properly understood, is a mode of creation. Atonement is an aspect of God's *ongoing* creative work. And God's redemptive commitment to continually re-creating us, to giving us a second life and a second birth, is definitively displayed in the person of Jesus Christ.

> But now, apart from law, the righteousness of God has been disclosed, and is attested by the law and the prophets, the righteousness of God through faith in Jesus Christ for all who believe. For there is no distinction, since all have sinned and fall short of the glory of God; they are now justified by his grace as a gift, through the redemption that is in Christ Jesus, whom God put forward as a sacrifice of atone-

---

5. Dieter F. Uchtdorf, "The Gift of Grace," LDS General Conference, April 2015, available at https://www.lds.org/general-conference/2015/04/the-gift-of-grace.

ment by his blood, effective through faith. He did this to show his
righteousness, because in his divine forbearance he had passed over
the sins previously committed; it was to prove at the present time that
he himself is righteous and that he justifies the one who has faith in
Jesus. (Rom. 3:21–26)

Paul poses Christ as the one who "discloses" God's righteousness. Christ
displays God's unconditional love for us and he does this "apart from
the law." As these verses describe it, Christ doesn't redeem us with his
blood by appeasing the judicial demands of a broken law. He doesn't
balance a deficit in obedience by complying with the law for us. Rather,
Christ redeems us by fulfilling the law and he fulfills the law by except-
ing himself from the law's jurisdiction, by accomplishing the end of
the law—love—without being compelled by the law to do so. Christ's
sacrifice doesn't confirm the law's inviolable priority. His sacrifice reveals exactly the opposite: that God's love is, rather, what is "attested *by
the law*" (Rom. 7:21, emphasis mine). Love doesn't bear witness to the
priority of the law, the law bears witness to the priority of love. The law
is given for the sake of love—and only love, uncompelled by the law,
can fulfill that law.

More, in this way, Christ's sacrifice doesn't bring into play some
kind of supplementary grace that was previously lacking or withheld,
that God was previously unwilling to give until an act of book-bal-
ancing obeisance had been made. Christ saves us from sin—from our
active suppression of God's grace—by displaying in an incomparable
fashion the very thing we had sinfully been trying to hide by hijacking
the law: the fact that God's grace is already and overwhelmingly available. Displaying what we'd suppressed, Christ gives *again* the grace of
creation (and re-creation) that God was already giving. Then, when we
are willing to recognize and receive God's sometimes terrifying grace,
we, too, are recreated with Christ. Loved by God through Christ, we
become capable of love.

Recreated by Christ, reborn in his image and bearing now his name
rather than our own, we, like Christ, experience a profound shift in our
relation to the law. We, like Christ, no longer live under the jurisdiction
of the law. And, now, no longer compelled by the law, we, too, become
capable of fulfilling it. As Paul puts it, with Christ we die to the law:

Do you not know, brothers and sisters—for I am speaking to those
who know the law—that the law is binding on a person only dur-

ing that person's lifetime? Thus a married woman is bound by the law to her husband as long as he lives; but if her husband dies, she is discharged from the law concerning the husband. Accordingly, she will be called an adulteress if she lives with another man while her husband is alive. But if her husband dies, she is free from that law, and if she marries another man, she is not an adulteress.

In the same way, my friends, you have died to the law through the body of Christ, so that you may belong to another, to him who has been raised from the dead in order that we may bear fruit for God. While we were living in the flesh, our sinful passions, aroused by the law, were at work in our members to bear fruit for death. But now we are discharged from the law, dead to that which held us captive, so that we are slaves not under the old written code but in the new life of the Spirit. (Rom. 7:1–6)

We die to the law through the body of Christ. We are crucified with him. Crucified with him, we become nothing. And, acknowledging our nothingness, we become, like Moses, the sons and daughters and God. No longer bound by the law that held us captive, we are free, like the widow, to love again. And, no longer bound by the law, we are free, in particular, to *fulfill* that law, like Christ, through love.

Given that the end of the law is love, the law can only be fulfilled by becoming an exception to the law. As long as we are subject to the law, the law cannot be fulfilled. But free from the jurisdiction of the law, the risk—as Paul is well aware—is antinomianism. The risk is that we will confuse our license to love with a license to sin. The risk is that, no longer bound by the law, we will simply leave the law unfulfilled. Consider the following chart:

	Subject to the Law	Exception to the Law
Law is Fulfilled	Ø	The Christian
Law is Unfulfilled	The Recognized Sinner	The Antinomian

There are, here, four possible positions in relation to the law. Vertically, we have two positions that are subject to the law and two positions that are exceptions to the law. Horizontally, we have two positions that fulfill the law and two positions that leave the law unfulfilled. The first position, the position that fulfills the law while being subject to the law, is an empty set. Not even Christ occupies this position because perfect compliance with the law cannot produce the kind of freely offered love that, alone, fulfills the law. This first position is empty not just because we are sinners—otherwise Christ could occupy it—but because of the catch-22 that structures the law. The second position is the position of the recognized sinner. The sinner lives under the jurisdiction of the law while failing to fulfill the law. The hallmark of this position is guilt. The third position is the position of the antinomian, the libertine who, operating outside the jurisdiction of the law, still does not fulfill the law. But the fourth position is the Christian position. Like Christ, the Christian operates outside the jurisdiction of the law. The Christian is an exception to the law and their position is not defined by obedience. But, like Christ, the Christian is now empowered by Christ's love to fulfill the law without compulsion.

Note, especially, how both the first and third positions shadow the Christian position with counterfeit versions of redemption. The first position offers the illusion of salvation *from grace* by way of a perfect obedience that would free us from dependence on God. The third position offers the illusion of salvation *from the law* without the trouble of love. But the fourth position, the Christian position, is capable of fulfilling the law by way of love precisely because it is an exception to the law. Neither counterfeit version should be allowed to impinge on the necessity of what they parody. Love is real, and God's grace shines through the whole of creation. Exposing ourselves to this grace—trusting this grace, exercising faith in what is given—the law will, as Nephi says, "become dead unto us" while we, still, are "made alive in Christ because of our faith" (2 Ne. 25:25).

5. Be Ye Perfect

What does this kind of Christian life look like? What would it mean to live in a way that fulfills the law without being subject to the law? What would it mean to live without flinching in the face of our own nothingness and the immensity of God's grace?

Dying to the law and living in Christ, we begin to carry ourselves with a characteristic grace, we begin to receive whatever is given with graciousness, and the whole of creation, regardless of its troubles, limitations, or transience, acquires a kind of perfection. The world becomes perfect in the same way that God is perfect. It becomes perfect in love.

> You have heard that it was said, "You shall love your neighbour and hate your enemy." But I say to you, Love your enemies and pray for those who persecute you, so that you may be children of your Father in heaven; for he makes his sun rise on the evil and on the good, and sends rain on the righteous and on the unrighteous. For if you love those who love you, what reward do you have? Do not even the tax-collectors do the same? And if you greet only your brothers and sisters, what more are you doing than others? Do not even the Gentiles do the same? Be perfect, therefore, as your heavenly Father is perfect. (Matt. 5:43–48)

Loving the neighbor is not enough. Loving those who love us—returning what is good to those who have already been good to us, fulfilling our legal obligations *quid pro quo*—is not enough. Our love must be practiced with a kind of disregard for the law. A perfect love is lawless in the way that God's love is lawless: a perfect love loves its enemies. Like God's love, this love isn't partial or divided or intermittent. It doesn't play favorites. God's love is, rather, impartial: it is whole or complete or perfect (*teleios*). It doesn't cease to give itself. It doesn't circumscribe its field. This love is like the sun: it shines on the evil and on the good. This love is like the rain: it rains on the just and unjust.

This love is, as John indicates, fearless. And, because it is fearless, this love becomes capable of grace. It becomes capable of receiving what it didn't want. It becomes capable of receiving its enemies. And, more, it becomes capable of returning to God what it did want and hoped to keep. It becomes capable of parting with its friends. No longer terrified by grace, this kind of love doesn't suppress the truth. It greets the world with an open hand. It receives creation. It doesn't regret the fact that much of what the world gives isn't what it would have liked and, in particular, it doesn't regret the fact that God can only continue to give more by taking back, at least in part, what he has already given. This kind of love can abide in grace because—beyond whatever the law could possibly require—it loves God and his gifts even when those gifts show up at the door as enemies.

Chapter 2

Burnt Offerings: Reading 1 Nephi 1

1. Lehi in the Desert

Where is Lehi going? What is he aiming to do? And, then, when the fire comes, what does he see and what does he hear?

We have only a handful of sentences. We know only the few details Nephi chooses to tell. And, to be fair, Nephi is trying to tell the story of his own life, not his father's—though, like all of us, he can only tell his story by abridging his father's life into his own. So, when the narration begins in the first chapter of 1 Nephi, Nephi begins with his father's story. On Nephi's account, his father's story starts midway through life. Already a grown man, already a father with children who are themselves almost grown, Lehi's story starts "in the commencement of the first year of the reign of Zedekiah, king of Judah" (1 Ne. 1:4).[1] This is useful information, but Nephi is not especially interested in kings. He's just setting the stage. Rather, he's interested in how, "in that same year there came many prophets prophesying unto the people that they must repent or the great city Jerusalem must be destroyed" (v. 4).

It's in response to these prophets that Lehi gets moving. Their words seem to shake loose some previously fixed part of him. So Lehi goes out. "Wherefore it came to pass that my father Lehi, as he went forth, prayed unto the Lord, even with all his heart, in behalf of his people" (v. 5). As he will frequently do in the verses that follow (cf. vv. 5, 6, 12, 14), Nephi's narration layers his father's actions, one on top of another. He narrates two things as happening at the same time: *as* Lehi

---

1. All citations of 1 Nephi in this essay refer to Royal Skousen's critical edition of the Book of Mormon, *The Book of Mormon: The Earliest Text* (New Haven: Yale University Press: 2009).

is going forth, Nephi says, he is *also* praying. In this verse, the layering of action conveys a sense of urgency. It gives the impression that there's no time for Lehi to stop and pray. Even while he's still going forth, he's already praying.

Where is Lehi going in such a hurry? Nephi doesn't say. But we can make a fair guess.

On Nephi's account, Lehi's "going forth" is explicitly linked to his hearing the call to repent. "There came many prophets prophesying unto the people that they must repent," Nephi says, "*wherefore . . .* my father Lehi, as he went forth, prayed." This "wherefore" implies a direct connection between Lehi's hearing the call to repent and his going forth. And more, by way of additional confirmation, we're told that, as he's going forth, Lehi is already pleading on behalf of his people. Lehi, it seems safe to say, is going out to pray and repent. He's going somewhere to plead for forgiveness. And for Lehi, the ritual procedure for doing so would be clear. The protocol for his time and place is that, in order to repent, he needs to offer sacrifice. Lehi needs to make a burnt offering.

In Hebrew, the technical term for a burnt offering is *korban olah* (literally, "an offering that goes up [in smoke]"). Such sin offerings are made by slaughtering an animal (a bull, a ram, a goat, turtle doves, or pigeons), sprinkling its blood on the altar, and then burning the flesh on an altar of unhewn stones until only ashes remain. In order to offer this sacrifice, standard procedure—especially after Josiah's centralizing reforms—would have sent Lehi to the temple in Jerusalem where priests and professionals could officiate on his behalf. But, for whatever reason, it appears that Lehi is headed *away* from Jerusalem because Nephi will later describe Lehi as having "*returned* to his own house at Jerusalem" after his first vision (1 Ne. 1:7, emphasis mine). We also know that once Lehi leaves Jerusalem with his family in chapter two, he won't hesitate to offer sacrifices outside the purview of the official temple cult: "And it came to pass that when he had traveled three days in the wilderness, he pitched his tent in a valley beside a river of water. And it came to pass that he built an altar of stones, and he made an offering unto the Lord and gave thanks unto the Lord our God" (2:7). Lehi appears comfortable building his own altar and officiating in his own rituals.

But if Lehi's not going up to the temple to offer sacrifice, then where is he going? My thesis is that Lehi is headed into the desert. I suggest that, like the prophets before him and, even, like Jesus after him, Lehi heard the voice of the Lord and then, having heard it, "immediately the spirit driveth him into the wilderness" (Mark 1:12). And now, having gone off into the desert, I think Lehi aims to offer sacrifice. I think he means to build a stone altar and make a burnt offering. If this is right, then how far into the desert does Lehi go? And how long is he out there? A day? Three days? Forty?

The Judean desert is harsh and empty. It slopes away to the east of Jerusalem and ends with steep cliffs that border the Dead Sea. The ground between is broken and mountainous. It's full of chalky hills and terraced plateaus cut by deep, wandering ravines. Imagine, now, Lehi deep in these rolling, bone-dry hills, alone for days, piling up stones for an altar. Imagine Lehi slaughtering a ram, flaying its skin, up to his elbows in gore, sprinkling its blood around the edges of the altar, and then praying with desperate grief on behalf of his people, praying until, as Nephi recounts it, "there came a pillar of fire and dwelt upon a rock before him, and he saw and heard much. And because of the things which he saw and heard, he did quake and tremble exceedingly" (1 Ne. 1:6). Once the vision arrives, its opening is dramatic enough that it leaves Lehi quaking, trembling, and exhausted.

But the vision's *form* probably shouldn't come as a surprise: Lehi sees a pillar of fire. And if Lehi is deep in the desert burning a sacrifice on an altar of piled stones, then the appearance of a pillar of fire on a rock is a good fit.[2] More, it's a good fit with precedent. Whether the pillar of fire is an extension of a fire that Lehi himself sets burning or whether it falls from heaven in dramatic fashion, the result is the same: God's presence is manifest.

There are four recorded occasions in the Old Testament when a pillar of fire falls from heaven to consume a sacrifice right on the altar.

1. God sends fire for Moses and Aaron in Leviticus 9:23–24: "And Moses and Aaron went into the tabernacle of the congregation, and came out, and blessed the people: and the glory of the Lord appeared unto all the people. And there came a fire out from before the Lord, and consumed upon the altar the burnt offering and the fat."

2. Fire falls from heaven for Solomon in 2 Chronicles 7:1–2: "Now when Solomon had made an end of praying, the fire

---

2. I'm indebted to Joseph Spencer for making this connection explicit.

came down from heaven, and consumed the burnt offering and the sacrifices; and the glory of the Lord filled the house. And the priests could not enter into the house of the Lord, because the glory of the Lord had filled the Lord's house."

3. Heavenly fire intervenes for Samson's father and mother in Judges 13:19–20: "So Manoah took a kid with a meat offering, and offered it upon a rock unto the Lord: and the angel did wonderously; and Manoah and his wife looked on. For it came to pass, when the flame went up toward heaven from off the altar, that the angel of the Lord ascended in the flame of the altar."

4. And, most famously, fire falls from heaven for Elijah at the climax of his duel with the priests of Baal in 1 Kings 18:37–39: "Hear me, O Lord, hear me, that this people may know that thou art the Lord God, and that thou hast turned their heart back again. Then the fire of the Lord fell, and consumed the burnt sacrifice, and the wood, and the stones, and the dust, and licked up the water that was in the trench. And when all the people saw it, they fell on their faces: and they said, The Lord, he is the God; the Lord, he is the God."

In each of these four cases, the consuming fire indicates God's acceptance of the sacrifice and makes his presence manifest. We should remember, too, that Moses, of course, hears the Lord speak to him out of a burning bush and, even more to the point, that a pillar of fire travels with Moses and the Israelites as they wander in the wilderness. Out in the desert, "the LORD went before them by day in a pillar of a cloud, to lead them the way; and by night in a pillar of fire, to give them light" (Ex. 13:21).

Once Lehi's pillar of fire arrives, Nephi tells us that his father "saw and heard much" and that "because of the things which he saw and heard, he did quake and tremble exceedingly" (1 Ne. 1:6). What, then, does Lehi see and what does he hear? We don't know. Nephi reports only Lehi's response: seeing and hearing, Lehi quakes and trembles. And, more, he's overcome by what he sees and hears. "And it came to pass that he returned to his own house at Jerusalem. And he cast himself upon his bed, being overcome with the Spirit and the things which he had seen" (v. 7). Lehi is spent and, thus spent, he reaches a critical threshold. In this sense, this first of Lehi's two consecutive visions in 1 Nephi 1 feels preparatory. It harrows the ground of Lehi's soul. It readies his heart and mind for the planting of the word. In stark contrast to the detail, definition, and articulation of Lehi's second vision (vv. 8–15), this first vision is raw and inarticulate. Where the second vision is rich with symbols, thrones, heavenly choirs, divine messengers, shouts of praise, and prophetic books, this first vision feels primal and elemental. Here there's nothing but blood and stone and fire.

Now, again, we aren't told what Lehi see or hears, but the upshot seems clear. This first consuming vision hints darkly at the oracle of destruction ("woe unto Jerusalem"!) that will be clearly pronounced in the second. Staring into that fire, watching it consume his offering, Lehi would have felt in his bones the truth of what would later be articulated in the vision that follows: God will demand that he sacrifice everything because everything (like his burnt offering) is going to be consumed by fire falling from heaven. This fire may fall dramatically in a flash of lightning or it may devour all that he loves and lives for with the slow (but inevitable) burn of time—but, either way, he must sacrifice everything. Lehi has no choice. He must return everything to the Lord. He must give it all up and he must give it all back. For Lehi (as for all of us), the world, as he knows it, is going to end. Jerusalem is going to be destroyed.

Remember, in this connection, that there is one *other* relevant case of fire falling from heaven that we have yet to mention. And this last case of fire falling from heaven involves the destruction of Sodom and Gomorrah.

> Then the Lord rained upon Sodom and upon Gomorrah brimstone and fire from the Lord out of heaven; and he overthrew those cities, and all the plain, and all the inhabitants of the cities, and that which grew upon the ground. . . . And Abraham gat up early in the morning to the place where he stood before the Lord: and he looked toward Sodom and Gomorrah, and toward all the land of the plain, and beheld, and, lo, the smoke of the country went up as the smoke of a furnace. (Gen. 19: 24–25, 27–28)

Lehi's visions are an apocalypse. He sees the end of the world and he sees, too, that the world's conflagration is both already underway and unavoidable. This world is passing away.

There is no avoiding it. *Either* (1) fire will fall from heaven to consume your sacrifice and manifest God's presence, *or* (2) fire will rain down from heaven to leave your city a smoking ruin. But have no doubt, everything will be consumed either way. As a result, Lehi only has two options. He can either *willingly* sacrifice his home, his people, his wealth, and his land, or he can cling to them and see them destroyed. The only question, here, is whether the world's consumption unfolds as a sacrifice or as a judgment. Will the pillar of fire be met with shouts of praise, a gesture of consecration, and an open hand? Or will it be met with fear, regret, and a closed fist?

In telling his father's story, Nephi means to demonstrate that the Lord can make those he has chosen "mighty, even unto the power of deliverance" and that his "tender mercies" are present and palpable for those faithful to him. But, along the way, Nephi also plainly demonstrates that the *kind* of deliverance God offers will consistently frustrate our expectations. Often, the promised deliverance works crosswise to our experience of loss and suffering and, in the main, it is a deliverance that comes to us *in* our afflictions rather than *from* them.

Lehi pleads with God in behalf of his people and God hears and answers his prayer. And Lehi rejoices in the promise that God's power and goodness and mercy are over all the earth and that the world will be redeemed. And still Lehi must leave everything and wander in the desert with his family and suffer great afflictions. And still the city of Jerusalem is destroyed.

2. Lehi with a Book

Let's turn, now, to a consideration of Nephi's account in this same chapter of Lehi's second vision. Ironically, the comparative wealth of information that Nephi gives us about Lehi's second vision works, in some respects, to make it even more mysterious than the initial encounter. Nephi's elisions and omissions, coupled with the vision's own internal logic of detour and delay, compound the mute opacity of the first.

Exhausted by the Spirit, Lehi returns home from his first vision to collapse on his bed. Overcome, he's carried away in a second vision that ratchets God's initial harrowing of Lehi's body a full turn deeper, down now into his heart and into his mind. "Being thus overcome with the Spirit, he was carried away in a vision, even that he saw the heavens open and he thought he saw God sitting upon his throne, surrounded with numberless concourses of angels in the attitude of singing and praising their God" (1 Ne. 1:8). Out of these open heavens, Lehi sees "one descending," followed by twelve others. The first is brighter than the sun at noonday. The twelve that follow are brighter than the stars.

The twelve scatter across the face of the earth but the first comes straight to Lehi and brings him a book. "And the first came and stood before my father, and gave unto him a book and bade him that he should read" (v. 11). In response, Lehi reads the text aloud and, as a result, he's filled again with the Spirit of the Lord.

Next, Nephi gives what seems to be our only direct quotation from the heavenly book itself, an oracle pronouncing judgment against Jerusalem: "Woe woe unto Jerusalem, for I have seen thine abominations" (v. 13). Nephi then moves directly to a swift summary of the book's remaining content: "Yea and many things did my father read concerning Jerusalem, that it should be destroyed and the inhabitants thereof; many should perish by the sword and many should be carried away captive into Babylon" (v. 13). Reacting to this oracle of woe, Lehi's response is surprising. Hearing it, he neither quakes nor trembles but instead shouts praises that, presumably, echo the songs of praise sung by the assembly of angels surrounding God's throne. "Great and marvelous are thy works, O Lord God Almighty," Lehi cries. "Thy throne is high in the heavens, and thy power and goodness and mercy is over all the inhabitants of the earth" (v. 14). Empowered to speak by the work of reading aloud, Lehi joins the heavenly choir, the divine council that is continually convened in the presence of God.

Note, now, a distinctive feature of this experience: there is in this vision quite a bit of what we might call "divine misdirection." Stepping back for a moment from an examination of what we *are* told by Nephi and what *is* given in the vision, we should also consider what we are *not* told and what God doesn't do. And when we do, surprising elisions and omissions (on Nephi's part) and apparently unnecessary detours and delays (on God's part) dominate the account. Consider, especially, one of the vision's most curious features: the fact that the whole of the vision pivots around a book that Lehi is asked to read. What is this book, and why is Lehi asked to read from it in the first place? The "one" who descends "out of the midst of heaven," whose "luster was above that of the sun at noonday," brings Lehi this book. Nephi never explicitly identifies who the one is—though, presumably, Nephi could have offered an interpretation, even if his father did not. Clearly, from our late perspective, "the one" is Christ and "the twelve" are his apostles. But it's not entirely clear, especially early on, how developed Lehi's own understanding of "a messiah" is. In some respects, Lehi's Christology appears at this point (perhaps unsurprisingly) relatively vague and un-developed. (We might compare, for instance, Lehi's vision of the tree of life with Nephi's expansive and detailed interpretation of that same dream.) What do we know about "the one" based just on the account? At least at the level of Nephi's narration, we're only told that "the one" descends "out of the midst of heaven" and that his "luster was above that of the sun at noonday." These two details make, I think, "the one's" most obvious prior point of reference the God who sits enthroned in the middle of the angelic throng.

But even apart from Nephi's reluctance to clearly identify "the one," a more important question remains: why, when the one arrives, does he bring Lehi a *book*? Why do we lack any account of the one communicating directly with Lehi? Why does the one descend from heaven in power and glory only to accomplish the mute handoff of a text? Why, if God is present *in person*, would that same God redirect Lehi's attention to the reading of a book? What's the point of this frustrating detour? Why have a text stand-in for God if God is there? Isn't the point of a divine text to connect you with God? Isn't the book a distraction in this instance? Or, at best, redundant? (It seems a bit like being in the same room as someone you love and, then, rather than addressing them directly, insisting that you only converse by way of telephone—or, better, insisting that, though you're standing face to face, all communication be routed only through a series of elliptical text messages!)

Similarly, what about two crucial features of this second vision that Nephi *could* have presented front and center but instead omits entirely from his initial summary: (1) his delayed report that "the things which [Lehi] read in the book, manifested plainly of the coming of a Messiah and also the redemption of the world" (1 Ne. 1:19), and (2) his delayed report of Lehi's actual prophetic commission (see 1 Nephi 2:1)? Why are we told about both of these things only in passing and only after the fact? The coming of a Messiah, the redemption of the world, and Lehi's explicit commission as a prophet aren't minor details. Rather, they ought to be at the center of the entire account.

Why all the detours and delays? Why all the omissions and elisions? I don't know.

But we can note, at least, that the imposition of such detours seems consonant with a much larger pattern. Take, for instance, the case of the Book of Mormon itself. Why go to the trouble of giving Joseph Smith the golden plates, have him translate that text with a method that hardly touches them, and then make the plates themselves disappear? Why force contemporary readers to detour through the text alone when solid evidence and a more direct connection seems possible? Why would God go out of his way to hide evidence and make his own (world-historically pivotal) message more obscure and less credible?

Or, even more to the point, what about God's own absence? Why put us in the same weak position as Lehi? Why give us a text, at least twice removed from God himself, rather than give us some kind of direct interaction with God? Is this a game or a test? Is God just testing us to see if we'll believe things that we don't have good evidence for? If this is the case, then what's God testing for, credulity? Is credulity the measure of a life, the litmus test for salvation? In effect, is God saying: "You're welcome to join me in eternal bliss, but only if you're willing to believe (in *exactly* the right way) things that I intentionally and unnecessarily made it really hard to understand and believe?"

I don't buy it. I don't buy this version of the story.

Life will surely test, at every turn, our willingness to be faithful to the hard work of caring for it, but life is not itself a cosmic pop quiz. And salvation, to whatever degree we're able to receive it, is not equivalent to getting a passing grade on your super-detailed, life-long report card.

What, then, is gained by all these detours and delays? Is there some reason why our deliverance from affliction and loss and suffering can't just directly and definitively be a deliverance from affliction and loss? Why (as for Lehi) must we suffer the forced choice of either willing sacrifice or devastating judgment? Why not provide a third option: freedom from all that trouble and delay in the first place?

3. The Mysteries of God

There are more questions here than answers. But, even without answers, the questions have force. At the very least, these questions work to bring more clearly into view what, in the very first verse of the very first chapter of the Book of Mormon, Nephi simply calls "the mysteries of God." The mysteries here in question are, on my reading, neither peripheral nor accidental. These mysteries are not an optional or temporary feature of the world. And it seems to me that, in the end, receiving God's grace and divine favor turns on our willingness to live our way *into* them.

God is, without a doubt, offering a real and present and palpable kind of deliverance from the losses and afflictions of life. But (and this is a big "but") the *kind* of deliverance he's offering appears to depart pretty sharply from the kind of deliverance we thought we wanted. We thought we wanted the golden plates, but God gives us a little blue paperback instead. We thought we wanted to talk directly with God, but God, even when he shows up in person, asks us to read something instead. We thought God might spare Jerusalem, but God asks us to willingly flee it instead.

The critical opening verse of the Book of Mormon (1 Ne. 1:1) reads as follows:

> I Nephi having been born of goodly parents, therefore I was taught somewhat in all the learning of my father. And having seen many afflictions in the course of my days, nevertheless having been highly favored of the Lord in all my days, yea having had a great knowledge of the goodness and the mysteries of God, therefore I make a record of my proceedings in my days.

Note, first, the relatively elaborate structure of the verse. The verse is structured by its two repetitions of the word "therefore" and its four repetitions of the word "having." On my reading, the verse's two "therefores," rather than its four "havings," are the key to its basic structure. If we give priority to the "therefores," then the verse makes two claims that have a distinctly causal structure:

(1) Having been born ... therefore I was taught.

(2) Having been afflicted ... therefore I make a record.

This causal "division of labor" (X therefore Y) is noteworthy. It's Nephi's being born that leads to his having been taught, but it's his having been afflicted that leads to his being compelled to write. His writing takes place as an inscription of his suffering. We're taught because we're born, he says, and we write (we order and record and narrate and inscribe) because we suffer.

However, it's the second claim that matters most here. To this point, I've compressed the complexity of the second claim in order to draw out its parallels with the first, but three of the verse's four "havings" belong to the second claim. Of the four repetitions, "having been born" belongs to the first claim, but "having seen many afflictions," "having been highly favored," and "having had a great knowledge" all belong to the second claim. On my reading, the third and fourth "havings" condition or qualify the second. (In fact, given the "yea" that punctuates the relationship of the third to the fourth "having," we might even read the fourth as an elaboration of the qualification initially made in the third.) We might represent the verse's structure like this:

(1) *having* been born of goodly parents,
<u>therefore</u> I was taught somewhat in all the learning of my father.

(2) and *having* seen many afflictions in the course of my days, nevertheless
    (a) *having* been highly favored of the Lord in all my days,
    (b) yea *having* had a great knowledge of the goodness and the mysteries of God,
<u>therefore</u> I make a record of my proceedings in my days.

Nephi's claim to have seen many afflictions in the course of his days is conditioned and qualified by his having been highly favored and having had great knowledge. And, most importantly, the relation of these two qualifications to his having seen many afflictions is structured by the verse's key term: Nephi's "nevertheless." "Having seen many afflictions, *nevertheless . . .*"

Theologically, this "nevertheless" is pivotal. Compare, for instance, Jesus's prayer in the garden of Gethsemane: "Father, if thou be willing, remove this cup from me: nevertheless not my will, but thine, be done" (Luke 22:42). Even given the fact that suffering and affliction condition the possibility of life and agency and love, *nevertheless* there is favor and goodness and knowledge. The nevertheless marks how favor and goodness and knowledge are all dependent upon the experience of suffering even as they are not reducible to it. The word marks how favor and goodness and knowledge aren't something detachable from loss and affliction but are, rather, dependent on a certain way of holding oneself in relationship to that suffering. This redemptive posture, this way of holding life's losses and passing, does not treat those losses simply as a negative, as a minus, as a "less." Rather, it holds life in such a way that divine favor and goodness and knowledge are not "less" (they are "never less") because of the afflictions. This recognition, the adoption of this posture in relation to suffering, is the heart of the gospel. It is what makes forgiveness and redemption possible.

In this respect, Nephi has been quite precise in this opening verse about what the mysteries of God involve. The mysteries of God have to do with this "nevertheless." To understand the mysteries of God is to understand how it is possible to see many afflictions *and* still be highly favored. This is the mystery: God's redemption doesn't involve an elimination of all suffering but a transformation of our relationship to that suffering such that the suffering itself becomes a condition of knowledge and favor.

Divine favor travels a path that runs parallel to the path of loss and affliction. Responding to God's call to repent, to sacrifice, and to consecrate doesn't involve switching from one track to the other, from the track of suffering to the track of divine favor. Rather, it involves our commitment to both, to holding life's losses together with Jesus's "nevertheless" in a way that acknowledges the reality of our failures and losses while still trusting that life *nevertheless* is good and beautiful. At times, the parallel line of deliverance bends and directly touches the line of affliction, freeing us from that particular trouble. But often (perhaps much more often), God is working at a more fundamental level to transform our natural posture in relation to loss and affliction from one of fear and refusal to one of love and responsibility. This is the divine mystery: freeing us entirely from loss and suffering—from the necessity of sacrificing everything—wouldn't free us from the troubles of life. It would only (and disastrously) free us from life itself.

The mystery is that having the golden plates available would not solve the real problem, that having God show up in person would not solve the real problem, and that freeing us from some particular affliction (while desirable in itself) would not solve the bigger problem. The facts of life and love inseparably entail loss and vulnerability. And the substance of both life and love is composed by the work this "nevertheless" does to weave life's afflictions and God's divine favor together. In this sense, the aim of the gospel isn't simply to give us what we think we want. Rather, its aim is to show us that what we thought we wanted isn't what God, in all his goodness and wisdom and mercy, is actually trying to give.

This essay was originally the product of a Mormon Theology Seminar co-sponsored with the Laura F. Willes Center for Book of Mormon Studies and the Neal A. Maxwell Institute for Religious Scholarship. The full collection of eight papers, A Dream, a Rock, and a Pillar of Fire: Reading 1 Nephi 1, *is currently forthcoming from the Maxwell Institute.*

Chapter 3

Reading Signs or Repeating Symptoms:
Reading Jacob 7

1. The Scene

Jacob and Sherem meet but they never connect. They circle the same sun but on wildly divergent planes. This isn't unusual. People talk past each other all the time. Our meetings are framed and spaced by layers of circumstance, ignorance, and protocol. The things that worry me are not the things that interest you. What you'd hope to see in me isn't the profile I wanted to show. And so we feel alone even when we're together.

Some of this is our own fault, but some of it isn't. Part of the problem is language itself. Language helps put us in relation, but it also structures those relations, and language, in order to be dependable, must be predictable. The way verbs are conjugated, the way words are ordered, the way certain kinds of statements or questions solicit a certain kind of response—these regularities give language its consistency. But these regularities also give language its rigidity. These words and forms give shape to the lives that we share but, too, the mechanical character of that language invests all of these ready-made words and prefabricated forms with a life of their own. They acquire an almost automatic character such that, rather than speaking a language, language often ends up speaking us.

Some of language's prefabricated forms are common and generic. Think of how greetings have a predictable formality. Or think of how the basic elements of a conversation between strangers at a party are already choreographed—the kinds of questions that can be asked, the kinds of answers that can be given. Most of what we say everyday is just a slight variation on what we said yesterday.

But some of these prefabricated forms are very specific to each person. These specific forms are shaped by the details of our personal histories, the idiosyncrasies of our genealogies, and, especially, by the constellations of need and desire that structured our earliest relationships. The patterns that structure these relationships—patterns that, to this day, situate me in a certain way with respect to my mother, that shape my expectations in relation to a friend, that make me hungry for my father's approval—these originally specialized patterns end up functioning as general templates for my relationships with other people.

These specialized patterns get recycled as all-purpose widgets and so I end up repeating with my boss elements of my relationship with my father, repeating with my wife elements of my relationship with my mother, repeating with my bishop elements of my relationship with my brother, etc. With some concretion, but generally with little awareness, these primal scenes get acted out again and again, automatically, mechanically, in my head, in my dreams, and in real life. At the heart of these scenes is a missing piece—a hole, a need—that fuels the drive to rigidly, symptomatically repeat them with whoever happens to be on hand.

Much of this repetition is futile: the hole never gets filled. But there is also a kind of utility here. Widely applied, the repetition of these scenes can make it easier to deal with people. Rather than needing to respond to the particulars, I can, without reflection, slot people into pre-assigned roles and then, focused on what I need, I can just respond to the generic features of the roles themselves. Rather than responding to you, I can respond to your role in the story I'm compelled—once again, today—to retell. In psychoanalysis this is called transference. In religion we often just call it sin. Sin: when we get bolted into patterns of transference that stubbornly keep us from seeing (and, thus, loving) someone else.

2. Jacob's Symptom

A lot of what happens between Jacob and Sherem in Jacob 7 has this feel. They talk right past each other. They can't quite see each other. They don't respond to each other as people but as types. Their projections lock orbits and their symptoms form a complementary pair.

Consider Jacob first. As Jacob narrates their encounter, the story has a stark, didactic simplicity. Jacob is good and Sherem is bad. Where Jacob displays "the power of the Lord" (Jacob 7:15), Sherem displays the "power of the devil" (v. 4).[1] On the face of it, this isn't wrong. But there is something disappointing about how this unfolds.

When Sherem confronts Jacob with a charge of blasphemy and perversion, Jacob responds in kind. Throughout, Jacob appears more interested in defending a certain kind of Christian doctrine than with enacting a certain kind of Christian behavior. He seems invested in and sharply limited by a certain pattern of speaking and thinking. To be sure, Sherem does the same with Jacob. But where this is predictable in Sherem's case, it feels tragic in Jacob's because the doctrine that Jacob is defending does itself maintain that Christian behavior is more important than any Christian ideas. The idea of Christ's love is not the thing at stake, Christ's love is. It's true that Jacob defends the idea of Christ's love with both force and effect, but it's also true that we hardly see him enacting that love.

Sherem, we're told, "lead away many hearts" from the doctrine of Christ (Jacob 7:3). But Jacob doesn't seek Sherem out. In fact, Sherem has to go looking for Jacob and, apparently, has a hard time finding him. Sherem, Jacob says, "sought much opportunity that he might come unto me" (v. 3). Where is Jacob? Why is he so hard to find? Why isn't he actively seeking out Sherem? Or, consider how things play out during and after their confrontation. When Sherem finds Jacob, he immediately levels an apparently sincere charge that Jacob's doctrine of Christ is perverting the law of Moses and misleading the people. Sherem sees himself as defending God's law. Jacob isn't impressed. He responds with some leading questions, invites God to smite Sherem as a sign, and then (wham!) "the power of the Lord came upon [Sherem], insomuch that he fell to the earth" (v. 15). But immediately following this sign, Jacob again disappears from the text and, in the aftermath, there is no mention of his being present to "nourish" Sherem as he lays stricken or of his being present to hear Sherem's deathbed confession. Essentially, Jacob shows up in the narrative only for the smiting itself.

Perhaps most telling, though, is Jacob's unquestioned confidence that Sherem's request for a sign is disingenuous. Jacob testifies that he knows, "by the power of the Holy Ghost," that "if there should be no atonement made, all mankind must be lost" (v. 12). Sherem asks for the

---

1. All citations of Jacob 7 in this essay refer to Royal Skousen's critical edition of the text, *The Book of Mormon: The Earliest Text*, (New Haven: Yale University Press: 2009).

same revelation: "Shew me a sign by this power of the Holy Ghost" (v. 13). But Jacob, without any hesitation, declares that, even if God were to show Sherem a sign, "yet thou wilt deny it because thou art of the devil" (v. 14). This is strong language and a boldly categorical prediction: even if the Holy Ghost were to intervene, Sherem will deny it, Jacob promises. There is no hope for Sherem.

But Jacob is wrong. The sign comes and—even though the sign comes in the form of a smiting—Sherem confesses Christ and repents. More, his testimony of Christ is sufficiently powerful that the multitude gathered to hear his testimony is "astonished exceedingly, insomuch that the power of God came down upon them and they were overcome, that they fell to the earth" (v. 21). In turn, this mass conversion is itself so profound that "the peace and love of God was restored again among the people" (v. 23). Sherem's deathbed preaching appears to be massively successful in a way that Jacob's own preaching was not.

But this isn't how Jacob frames it. Jacob undercuts any part Sherem may have had in sparking this transformation by claiming that all of the above happened because "I had requested it of my Father which was in heaven, for he had heard my cry and answered my prayer" (v. 22). Here, Jacob's prayers are assigned the role of prime mover and Sherem won't be allowed out of the box Jacob has put him in. And so, with a final parting jab, Jacob baldly concludes the whole story by *still* referring to Sherem as "this wicked man" (v. 23).

3. Sherem's Position

Much of Jacob's treatment of Sherem feels shortsighted and unfair. And though Jacob successfully defends the doctrine of Christ, he doesn't seem to do it in a very Christ-like way. In fact, he defends the doctrine of Christ against the letter of the Mosaic law in a way that, in itself, seems in lockstep with the letter of the law. What's going on here? If Jacob is slotting Sherem into a prefabricated role in a scene that Jacob's own life compels him to replay, what role is this? What position does Sherem occupy?

Something about Sherem sets Jacob off. Something about him reopens an old wound. Jacob clearly bears a such wound. Only moments after recounting his unmitigated victory over Sherem, Jacob drifts right back into melancholy and tells us that, until his dying day, he mourned:

"We did mourn out our days" (Jacob 7:26). What is the cause of Jacob's persistent mourning? Why can't he put it behind him? The Nephites, Jacob recounts, were "a lonesome and a solemn people, wanderers cast out from Jerusalem, born in tribulation in a wild wilderness, and hated of our brethren, which caused wars and contentions" (v. 26). Jacob is the bearer of this old wound, his father's wound, a family wound. He mourns for Jerusalem. He mourns for the loss of a city he never knew. But, for Jacob, this wound has some additional specificity. He is also "hated of his brethren," and this is not "brethren" in the abstract. As a first generation Nephite, Jacob means something much more immediate: he means his actual brothers, Laman and Lemuel.

Jacob's lonesome tribulation in the wilderness is framed on the one hand by the loss of a city he never knew and, on the other, by the fact that his brothers hate him. The catalyst for both these losses is the same: the doctrine of Christ. From the start, Nephi reports, the Jews hated and "did mock [Lehi] because of the things which he testified of them" because he "testified that the things which he saw and heard, and also the things which he read in the book, manifested plainly of the coming of a Messiah, and also the redemption of the world" (1 Ne. 1:19). And from the start, Nephi continues, Laman and Lemuel "were like unto [those] who were at Jerusalem" (2:13).

These are the lines that frame Jacob's primal scene. And this is the scene that will, with a telling mechanicity, repeat itself not only in Jacob's life but, for the next thousand years, in the bodies of his people— again and again, generation after generation—until the repetition itself destroys them all. When Jacob looks at Sherem, why can't he see him? I think the answer is straightforward. When Jacob looks at Sherem all he can see is Laman and Lemuel. He can't engage with Sherem because, throughout their encounter, he's too busy shadow-boxing his brothers.

Sherem, like Laman, Lemuel, and the people in Jerusalem, is a defender of the received tradition. In particular, Sherem, like Laman and Lemuel, is keen to defend the primacy of the law of Moses against the imposition of any novel dreams, visions, or messianic revelations. But these are, as Nephi noted, exactly the objections lodged by Laman and Lemuel against Lehi. "Thou art like unto our father," they tell Nephi, "led away by the foolish imaginations of his heart . . . we know that the people who were in the land of Jerusalem were a righteous people; for they kept the statutes and judgments of the Lord, and all his commandments, according to the law of Moses; wherefore we know that they are a righteous people" (1 Ne. 17:20, 22). Sherem mirrors exactly these claims:

> And ye have led away much of this people, that they pervert the right way of God and keep not the law of Moses, which is the right way, and convert the law of Moses into the worship of a being which ye say shall come many hundred years hence. And now behold, I Sherem declare unto you that this is blasphemy, for no man knoweth of such things; for he cannot tell of things to come. (Jacob 7:7)

On Sherem's account the "law of Moses" is itself the "right way of God," not a shadow of it, not a sign of things to come. For Sherem, Jacob's doctrine of Christ looks beyond the mark and ignores the plainness of the law. It "converts" the law of Moses into an apparatus for worshipping a future Messiah and, as a result, it interferes with the law's operation as what structures and orders our everyday lives and relationships.

It's on this score that Sherem's position is more consistent than Jacob's. Sherem's position that the law is what structures and orders our relationship to the world is consistent with his own willingness to submit to and massage the structures imposed by language. But Jacob's willingness to do the same is not consistent with the doctrine of Christ he's defending. Sherem is a master of the law. And, in particular, he is a master of how the law organizes our desires and locks us into repeating certain scenes. Sherem, Jacob tells us, "was learned, that he had a perfect knowledge of the language of the people; wherefore he could use much flattery and much power of speech according to the power of the devil" (Jacob 7:4). Sherem's learning and power are pegged directly to his "perfect knowledge of the language of the people." He understands how language works, he recognizes the constraints that language imposes, and he knows that, at the heart of our compulsion to repeat these primal scenes, is a wound, a need, a desire. Sherem recognizes these templates as symptoms. As a result, Sherem can position himself in a way that is flattering to the stories that people need to repeat.

This is what flattery amounts to: the power to position yourself as a willing mirror for whatever image others hope to see reflected back to them. In this sense, flattery isn't just a name for a certain way of speaking, it's a general name for smoothly functioning transference. When flattery succeeds, it creates order. It gathers people up. It stabilizes the images we project onto each other. Flattery shows us what we want to see. It reflects back to us what we expected. When this happens, a reassuring consistency reigns. But this compelled, mechanical consistency is also quite stifling and, ultimately, lonely. A regulated economy of mirror images is exhilarating but empty.

This is where Jacob and Sherem find themselves: hamstrung by flattery. They are compelled by their wounds to repeat complementary scenes, scenes that bind them together as a pair of prefabricated images but prevent them from connecting as people. Sherem doesn't address Jacob, he addresses only a "law-breaker." And Jacob doesn't address Sherem, he addresses only a "Christ-denier." Though adversarial, these roles collude to reinforce the mutual exclusion of the actual people attached to them.

4. Signs from Heaven

What, then, can be done? It's not as if we could do without these structures that order and regulate our relationships. It's not as if we could do without law and language. Without law and language we would be even more isolated and alone than we are when we're trapped within their confines. What we need, rather, is a doctrine of Christ that can enact a new relation to the law, a doctrine that can retain these structures but give us room to move in relation to them.

The key to this doctrine of Christ is a spirit of prophecy that can read the law itself as sign. Rather than just repeating it as a symptom, a spirit of prophecy can read in the staging of a primal scene the truth about the too-human wound that compels the repetition in the first place. This spirit can, as Jacob puts it, recognize that "none of the prophets have written nor prophesied save they have spoken concerning this Christ" (Jacob 7:11).

Now, at one level, what Jacob claims about scripture is clearly false. Most of scripture is straightforwardly, like the law itself, about something *other* than Christ. In order to point to Christ, the law and prophets must themselves be read as signs that, at heart, testify to the truth of the world's original wound and, especially, to the manifestation of Christ in that wound as the lamb slain from the foundation of the world (cf. Rev. 13:8). This is the doctrine of Christ:

> And, notwithstanding we believe in Christ, we keep the law of Moses, and look forward with steadfastness unto Christ, until the law shall be fulfilled. For, for this end was the law given; wherefore the law

hath become dead unto us, and we are made alive in Christ because of our faith; yet we keep the law because of the commandments. And we talk of Christ, we rejoice in Christ, we preach of Christ, we prophesy of Christ, and we write according to our prophecies, that our children may know to what source they may look for a remission of their sins. Wherefore, we speak concerning the law that our children may know the deadness of the law; and they, knowing the deadness of the law, may look forward unto that life which is in Christ, and know for what end the law was given. (2 Ne. 25:24–27)

The law must be kept and its structures preserved, but they must be kept in such a way that they become "dead unto us." When this happens, the spell is broken.

In sin, the law takes on a life of its own, and *we* feel dead in relation to it. We feel excluded from our own lives and isolated from other people. But the doctrine of Christ inverts this scenario. When the law becomes dead, when the law no longer has a life of its own, when it loses its automatic and mechanical character, then we discover a new life in Christ. We're freed from sin. We're no longer locked into repeating the same futile, bloodless scenes. The key, again, is that the law must start functioning as a sign. We have to learn to read the performance of these scenes not, like Sherem, as a symptom available for manipulation but, like a prophet, as a sign that displays the human wounds that animate them.

This is hard to do. The templates that structure our relationships are themselves a defensive gesture meant to compensate for the wound that compels them. But there is, here, a general lesson to be drawn from Sherem's own experience of a sign. When signs come, they inevitably come, to one degree or another, as they did for Sherem. As Jacob puts it: "if God shall smite thee, let that be a sign unto thee" (Jacob 7:14). Every sign is smiting. Every sign that reveals Christ reveals him by touching the wound that we were working to conceal. These signs break the tight circle of transference, of collusion and vanity. They collapse our prearranged games. They open us to something beyond the prefabricated scenes and ready-made meanings we work so hard to impose on the world. And they make room for these scenes to be redeployed, instead, as signs of the very wounds they'd been hiding. Signs open us to the possibility of revelation, ministering angels, prophecies, visions, and dreams. Signs, revealing the doctrine of Christ, open us to the possibility of a world where we are not alone.

5. Reclamation

In conclusion, allow me to speculate on a final point. When God smites Sherem such that he falls to the earth, this is a sign. But, it seems to me, this sign isn't just for Sherem. This sign is also meant for Jacob. Granted, the sign wakes Sherem up such that he "confessed the Christ and the power of the Holy Ghost and the ministering of angels" (Jacob 7:17). But the sign gives Jacob a bracing shake as well. It may be true that Jacob never truly sees Sherem—Sherem dies before they really have a chance—but Jacob clearly signals that, even if he never manages to see Sherem, Sherem has put him in a position to see Laman and Lemuel again.

Note that after Sherem confesses Christ and "the love of God" is restored among the people, Jacob immediately turns his attention to the Lamanites: "And it came to pass that many means were devised to reclaim and restore the Lamanites to the knowledge of the truth" (v. 24). These efforts fail, but the fact that Jacob is moved to *try* is significant. When he looked at Sherem, Jacob could only see the ghosts of Laman and Lemuel. He saw these ghosts so clearly that he was sure that even if God gave Sherem a sign, Sherem (like Laman and Lemuel) would harden his heart and never repent.

But the sign came and Sherem *did* repent. He did confess Christ. And then something happens to Jacob. For the first time in decades, Jacob can see his own brothers more clearly. He can see Laman and Lemuel, not as players in his story but as flesh and blood people. For the first time in decades, Jacob can read in their anger the wound that compelled *them* to repeat their own primal scene. Then, for the first time in decades, Jacob dares to hope that his brothers aren't lost forever. This is the doctrine of Christ.

This essay was originally the product of a Mormon Theology Seminar co-sponsored with the Laura F. Willes Center for Book of Mormon Studies and the Neal A. Maxwell Institute for Religious Scholarship. The full collection of seven papers, Christ and Antichrist: Reading Jacob 7, *is currently forthcoming from the Maxwell Institute.*

Chapter 4

Early Onset Postmortality

The good news, Paul announces, is that it's possible to die while you're still alive. It's possible to survive your own death and, remarkably, to be all the more alive for it. "I am crucified with Christ: nevertheless I live; yet not I, but Christ liveth in me: and the life which I now live in the flesh I live by the faith of the Son of God, who loved me, and gave himself for me" (Gal. 2:20). This is what salvation—not as a future event but as a present tense reality—looks like. To experience salvation is to experience *early onset postmortality*.

In early onset postmortality, you discover a time within time and your day of judgment arrives before your life ends. And then, in the time that remains between your final judgment and your final breath, you discover what it is like to be alive after death, to have faith persist beyond belief, and to have love abide on the far side of the law's fulfillment. Having passed redemption by, you now live a life that is no longer aimed somewhere else. No longer mortal but not yet immortal, you discover what it means to be human.

In *Moby Dick*, Melville recounts an instance of early onset postmortality. Ishmael, having barely survived his first lowering of the boats in pursuit of a whale, adds up the now palpable dangers involved in whaling and decides that, "taking all things together, I say, I thought I might as well go below and make a rough draft of my will. 'Queequeg,' said I, 'come along, you shall be my lawyer, executor, and legatee.'"[1] Then, Ishmael says, after his last will and testament had been drawn and sealed,

> after the ceremony was concluded on the present occasion, I felt all
> the easier; a stone was rolled away from my heart. Besides, all the days

---

1. Herman Melville, *Moby Dick* (New York: Modern Library, 1992), 331.

I should now live would be as good as the days that Lazarus lived after his resurrection; a supplementary clean gain of so many months or weeks as the case might be. I survived myself; my death and burial were locked up in my chest. I looked round me tranquilly and contentedly, like a quiet ghost with a clean conscience sitting inside the bars of a snug family vault.[2]

Like Lazarus, Ishmael has survived himself. He has already attended, Tom Sawyer-like, his own funeral. He has acquired a clean supplementary gain of so many months or weeks. And in the aftermath of his prevenient funeral, still breathing, the stone gets rolled away from his heart.

A playful exuberance takes hold and Ishmael is empowered to act with the kind of grace and freedom that the threat of death and judgment, while still pending, had denied him. He has become, like the gods, capable of laughter.

There are certain queer times and occasions in this strange mixed affair we call life when a man takes this whole universe for a vast practical joke, though the wit thereof he but dimly discerns, and more than suspects that the joke is at nobody's expense but his own. However, nothing dispirits, and nothing seems worth while disputing. He bolts down all events, all creeds, and beliefs, and persuasions, all hard things visible and invisible, never mind how knobby; as an ostrich of potent digestion gobbles down bullets and gun flints. And as for small difficulties and worryings, prospects of sudden disaster, peril of life and limb; all these, and death itself, seem to him only sly, good-natured hits, and jolly punches in the side bestowed by the unseen and unaccountable old joker.

That odd sort of wayward mood I am speaking of, comes over a man only in some time of extreme tribulation; it comes in the very midst of his earnestness, so that what just before might have seemed to him a thing momentous, now seems but a part of a general joke. There is nothing like the perils of whaling to breed this free and easy sort of genial, desperado philosophy; and with it I now regarded this whole voyage of the Pequod, and the great White Whale its object.[3]

Like Christ crucified, Ishmael can say, it is finished. And, like Christ, he now finds himself expansive. Outlasting his death, he's gripped by an earnest jocularity that is free of resentment and capable of swallowing

---

2. Ibid., 331.
3. Ibid., 329.

all events, creeds, and beliefs, no matter how angular or gnarly. He gulps down life and breathes its troubles with capacious lungs.

Though he still walks the earth, he has already passed by the pearly gates and entered the rest of the Lord. But having entered this rest, he doesn't stop. He takes the Sabbath with him and keeps on walking. He returns to his ordinary life and its ordinary business *as* a sabbatical. Having passed the point of judgment, having had all of his good and evil works already tallied in the book of life and having had that account closed, his work becomes play. His work becomes a grace.

In this sense, Ishmael is like John the Beloved or the Three Nephites. They are all living backdated lives. Their lives ended long ago and yet they're still wandering around, hitchhiking lonely roads, changing tires, and singing Christmas carols that the rest of us have forgotten.

Or, better, early onset postmortality is like what Mormons call "having your calling and election made sure." This is the model: you're not dead yet, but your day of judgment arrives nonetheless. God has seen enough. Your life is to be rolled up like a scroll, sealed with a stamp, and returned to you to do with as you wish—just don't murder or blaspheme the Holy Ghost. *Mormon Doctrine* summarizes the point like this:

> Thus, as the Prophet also said, "The more sure word of prophecy means a man's knowing that he is sealed up unto eternal life, by revelation and the spirit of prophecy, through the power of the Holy Priesthood." (D&C 131:5) Those so favored of the Lord are sealed up against all manner of sin and blasphemy except the blasphemy against the Holy Ghost and the shedding of innocent blood. That is, their exaltation is assured; their calling and election is made sure, because they have obeyed the fullness of God's laws and have overcome the world. Though such persons "shall commit any sin or transgression of the new and everlasting covenant whatever, and all manner of blasphemies, and if they commit no murder wherein they shed innocent blood, yet they shall come forth in the first resurrection, and enter into their exaltation." (D&C 132:26)[4]

When your calling and election are made sure, life jumps its eschatological track and things start happening out of order. Instead of being postponed until the next life, redemption arrives early. Judgment passes

---

4. Bruce R. McConkie, *Mormon Doctrine*, 2d ed. (Salt Lake City: Bookcraft, 1966), 109–10.

proleptically, you finish with the law, and your resurrection gets underway before you've even finished dying.

Moreover, despite Mormonism's typical treatment of them, such things are not meant to be rare. Having one's calling and election made sure just models in dramatic fashion what ordinary repentance, forgiveness, and life in Christ were meant to look like all along. Repentance—regular, average, everyday repentance—*is* the practice of early onset postmortality. When you repent, you confess your disobedience. You embrace the law and stop running from it. You step into rather than away from its embrace. Repenting, you submit a request for a speedy verdict and ask for judgment now rather than later. But stepping into the law, your relationship to the law's demands shift. Rather than living as if your life were given for the sake of the law, you discover that the law was given for the sake of life. You were not made for the Sabbath, the Sabbath was made for you (cf. Mark 2:27). And the law, rather than working as an instrument of condemnation, is rendered inoperative by an excess of grace that both suspends and fulfills it.

You assume a new relation to the law and the law, already fulfilled by Christ, becomes dead to you. Or, better, *you* become dead to the law. The grace enacted and received in repentance is meant to initiate you into the messianic secret. And the messianic secret is this: that there is a time *within* time, a time that fulfills the law without being subject to it, a time where your death, though still on its way, is already passed and toothless.

In *The Time That Remains: A Commentary on the Letter to the Romans*, Giorgio Agamben reads Paul's letter as an extended commentary on this messianic secret and the grace that attends early onset postmortality. The model for what Agamben calls messianic time is that peculiar time—that remnant of time that remains—following the accomplishment of the messianic event but preceding the end of time. On this score, Agamben argues, Paul is not a prophet but an apostle. "The prophet is essentially defined through his relation to the future" and "each time the prophets announce the coming Messiah, the message is always about a time to come, a time not yet present."[5] But, Agamben argues, Paul speaks not as a prophet about a future event, but as an apostle about the present unveiling of a salvation that, despite history's failure to end, has already arrived. "The apostle speaks forth from the arrival of

---

5. Giorgio Agamben, *The Time That Remains: A Commentary on the Letter to the Romans* (Stanford: Stanford University Press, 2005), 61.

the Messiah. At this point prophecy must keep silent, for now prophecy is truly fulfilled. . . . This is why Paul's technical term for the messianic event is *ho nyn kairos*, 'the time of the now.'"[6] In this sense, an apostle's job is to evangelize early onset postmortality.

The key to understanding Paul's letter, Agamben contends, is to recognize that messianic time (*kairos*) is not some time outside of or opposed to ordinary secular time (*chronos*). If that were the case, secular time would have already come to an end. But secular time, despite the accomplishment of the decisive messianic event, despite Christ's resurrection, has continued along just as before. Rather, the force of the messianic event resides in its capacity to reveal messianic time as a kind of time that has always already been at work *in* secular time, simultaneously disrupting and composing it from within.

Messianic time testifies to the impossibility of any simple secular history. And, more, it announces a complex temporality that harbors the possibility of repentance. Drawing on Gustave Guillaume's account of "operational time," Agamben describes messianic time as the time it takes for a temporal representation to be accomplished. Secular time, on the other hand, is a homogenous time composed of *completed* representations. It "presents time as though it were always already constructed, but does not show time in the act of being constructed."[7] More:

> In order to truly understand something, Guillaume says, considering it only in its constructed or achieved state is not enough; you also have to represent the phases through which thought had to pass constructing it. Every mental operation, however quick, has to be achieved in a certain time, which, while short, is no less real. Guillaume defines "operational time" as *the time the mind takes to realize a time-image.*[8]

In this sense, all secular time implies a second time that cannot be included within the scope of its finished representation: this second time is the time necessary to complete the secular's own construction. This second "operational" time names a time within time that complicates and disrupts secular time, even as it gives it. Operational time is the time that remains unaccounted for once secular time has added up everything else.

Consider a photo of the night sky. The photo documents in one stroke a simple, contemporaneous image of light shining from stars. But

---

6. Ibid.
7. Ibid., 65.
8. Ibid., 65–66.

the simplicity of the accomplished image masks the complex temporality at work in its construction. It masks the time lag (the operational time) that makes it possible. Here, such lag is dramatic and can be measured in terms of the millions of years it took for that star light to reach us. A photo of the night sky is shot through with operational time.

This last point is obvious, but it should also be obvious that this same operational lag is at work in *all* of our experiences, though often on a micro scale. The time it takes for sound to travel, for light to arrive, for meaning to be constructed, for experience to be assembled, for the mind to think a thought, for a declaration of love to be understood, etc. These things have a price; they take time to complete.

Secular time is both dependent on and riven with a complex temporality working on countless overlapping scales, both micro and macro, that it cannot master or include in its own representations. More, as Agamben observes:

> In the firmament that we observe at night, the stars shine brightly, surrounded by a thick darkness. Since the number of galaxies and luminous bodies in the universe is almost infinite, the darkness that we see in the sky is something that, according to scientists, demands an explanation. . . . In an expanding universe, the most remote galaxies move away from us at a speed so great that their light is never able to reach us. What we perceive as the darkness of the heavens is this light that, though traveling towards us, cannot reach us, since the galaxies from which the light originates move away from us at a velocity greater than the speed of light. To perceive, in the darkness of the present, this light that strives to reach us but cannot—that is what it means to be contemporary. As such, contemporaries are rare.[9]

The darkness of the night sky is full of light, but it is full of a light that cannot reach us *in time* to be included in the image.

(As a side note, it seems to me that the receding temporality of this dark light proper to operational time may be the key to understanding the peculiar character of the Book of Mormon's own profoundly irregular brand of historicity. We cannot meaningfully approach questions about the Book of Mormon's historicity without a clear account of the complex temporality proper to its messianic work. The Book of Mor-

---

9. Giorgio Agamben, *Nudities* (Stanford: Stanford University Press, 2010), 14–15.

mon recedes from us at a speed so great that the light of its historicity, while always on its way, cannot reach us.)

Operational time is this dark light, this temporal remnant, this time tucked inside of time, that renders our image of the heavens fragile and outdated and incomplete. To experience early onset postmortality is to be displaced out of time's completion in the faux-sufficiency of a secular image and into the freedom of this dark light. Another way to say this is that operational time, this time that remains, is the remnant of time that is left once secular history has exhausted itself in actuality. Operational time, as messianic time, is what makes room for an early onset post-*secularity*.

The messianic takes advantage of time's complexity, of the time within time, of the potential that has not exhausted itself in the actual, of the light still traveling toward us in darkness, for the sake of life and repentance. Rather than being linear, the inclusion of operational time in our account of history and temporality renders time complex and three-dimensional and puts us in relation not just to time's *product* but to the power inherent in time's ongoing, present-tense *production*—the supercharged fullness of time.

The messianic depends on the fact that the end can pass without time having been used up. To experience redemption is to experience time from the perspective of this temporal remnant rather than from the perspective of secular history. It is to experience history's point of origin as located in an open present rather than in a closed past. It is to experience life from the perspective of the potential that constitutes but is never exhausted in the actual. It is to experience life as a present-tense ongoing power of creation rather than an accomplished past tense event. It is to experience the past as incomplete, as uncompleted by the operational time it could not incorporate, and the present as overflowing with a fullness that it cannot contain.

Messianic time is this fullness of time in which redemption has already passed and life, both irrepressible and irreparable, continues on anyway. As Agamben says, "messianic time is neither the complete nor the incomplete, neither the past or the future, but the inversion of both."[10]

> The Messiah has already arrived, the messianic event has already happened, but its presence contains within itself another time, which stretches its *parousia*, not in order to defer it, but, on the contrary, to

10. Agamben, *Time That Remains*, 75.

make it graspable. For this reason, each instant may be, to use Benjamin's words, the "small door through which the Messiah enters."[11]

Messianic time, as the Sabbath, as a sabbatical day of rest, "is not another day, homogeneous to others; rather, it is that innermost disjointedness within time through which one may—by a hairsbreadth—grasp time and accomplish it."[12]

Passing through the messianic gate of time's innermost disjointedness, you see that the past was made for the sake of the present, not the present for the sake of the past. In other words, you repent. Repentance is only possible if time is complex and the past persists unfinished, kept alive beyond itself by a remnant of time that no amount of pride or sinful pretension to self-possession could smother.

This reading of Paul pivots around a passage from 1 Corinthians 7:29–32. Agamben's translation of these verses reads as follows:

> But this I say, brethren, time contracted itself, the rest is, that even those having wives may be as not [*hos me*] having, and those weeping as not weeping, and those rejoicing as not rejoicing, and those buying as not possessing, and those using the world as not using it up. For passing away is the figure of the world. But I wish you to be without care.[13]

In the rest of the time that remains, Agamben argues, God's call to each of us is to accept a messianic vocation.

This messianic vocation is not, however, like any normal vocation. It does not ask us, as subjects, to link our lives to any particular qualities or vocation—that is, what Agamben calls "predicates." Rather, it asks us to take up whatever secular predicates already define us (tall, teacher, male, Caucasian, father, Mormon, whatever) *in a new and peculiarly messianic way*. The messianic vocation operates as an only partial revocation of our secular vocations, of our ordinary predicates. It asks us to treat those secular vocations and secular predicates *as if they were not*, as if they were no longer in force: "those having wives may be as not having, and those weeping as not weeping, and those rejoicing as not rejoicing." "According to the principle of messianic [calling]," Agamben writes, each "determinate factical condition is set in relation to itself—the weeping is pushed toward the weeping, the rejoicing toward the

---

11. Ibid., 71.
12. Ibid., 72.
13. Ibid., 23.

rejoicing. In this manner, it revokes the factical condition and under-mines it without altering its form."[14] Or, as Agamben puts it elsewhere: "To be messianic, to live in the Messiah, signifies the expropriation of each and every juridical-factical property (circumcised/uncircumcised; free/slave; man/woman) under the form of the *as not*. This expropria-tion does not, however, found a new identity; the 'new creature' is none other than the use and messianic vocation of the old."[15]

To enter your messianic vocation and begin a life in Christ means (1) that the governing force of the laws and predicates that defined your secular life has been revoked, that your life has ended, but also (2) that despite their revocation you go on living just as before, just as you'd pre-viously been. Your predicated life has ended, but you go on performing these predications nonetheless.

As a result, perhaps for the first time, things become just "whatever they are." Things are free to be perfectly whatever kind of thing they ordinarily are. The world is graced not by a flawlessness but by a halo of perfection that shines from the world's no longer being a means to some other end, to someplace else. It has, instead, become something to be loved, as it is, for its own sake. This work of love—of a perfect love that does not fear imperfection—is the essence of the messianic voca-tion. It is the work to be done in the time that remains.

By way of conclusion, let's return for a moment to *Moby Dick*. Late in the book, Queequeg, sick on his deathbed, asks the ship's carpenter to fashion him a burial canoe. Once it is fashioned, Queequeg demands to try it out, laying himself the length of it, testing its virtue. Lying still as a stone in his own coffin, he looks like he's already dead. Then, hav-ing abruptly remembered some small, ordinary task he'd forgotten to do, Queequeg jumps up out of the coffin and returns from the grave. "With a wild whimsiness," Melville tells us, "he now used his coffin for a sea-chest; and emptying into it his canvas bag of clothes, set them in order there."[16]

> Many spare hours he spent, in carving the lid with all manner of gro-tesque figures and drawings; and it seemed that hereby he was striv-ing, in his rude way, to copy parts of the twisted tattooing on his body. And this tattooing, had been the work of a departed prophet and seer

---

14. Ibid., 24.
15. Ibid., 26.
16. Melville, *Moby Dick*, 690.

of his island, who, by those hieroglyphic marks, had written out on his body a complete theory of the heavens and the earth, and a mystical treatise on the art of attaining truth; so that Queequeg in his own proper person was a riddle to unfold; a wondrous work in one volume; but whose mysteries not even himself could read, though his own live heart beat against them; and these mysteries were therefore destined in the end to moulder away with the living parchment whereon they were inscribed, and so be unsolved to the last. And this thought it must have been which suggested to Ahab that wild exclamation of his, when one morning turning away from surveying poor Queequeg —"Oh, devilish tantalization of the gods!"[17]

This is the claim: that some departed prophet and seer of your own island has left, tattooed round the circumference of your flesh, a spiraling revelation, a promise of forgiveness, a complete theory of repentance, a mystical treatise on the art of attaining truth, a riddle in your own proper person to unfold, a messianic text inscribed in your flesh. This prophet came and went long before you arrived.

The tattoos are meant for you, a kind of story of your life inscribed within your life, but you're going to have to die young in order to read them. Order your coffin, lay the length of it and let your life end, die to this world, leave it behind—and then remember that you've forgotten to wash a dish or kiss your wife or sweep the porch or read to your child. Then leap from your coffin and return in earnest to the work of washing and kissing and sweeping and reading, sure and fearless in the time that remains.

17. Ibid., 690–91.

Chapter 5

The God Who Weeps:
Notes, Amens, and Disagreements

The God Who Weeps is a different kind of book. It's devotional in spirit but academic in pedigree. It's published by Deseret Book but under its Ensign Peak imprint. It's an aggressively expansive book that, instead of quoting general authorities, ranges across the whole Western tradition, skillfully absorbing and repurposing whatever stories and ideas speak to its Mormon ears. It's a book that matters because, rather than asking us to agree, it asks us to think.

It's importance depends on this difference. In order for *Weeps* to make a lasting difference—and I think it can and should—it needs to be different enough for us to care. If its ideas are too similar (or dissimilar) to what we usually say, then its influence will be limited. But if its account of Mormonism is just different enough to simultaneously prompt a moment of recognition *and* motivate a cascade of thoughtful disagreement, then its influence will radiate. On the other hand, if the book prompts only assent, I worry that a chorus of amens will silence it.

Weeps is invigorating precisely because it does not mime the voice of authority. It speaks and thinks in its own name. We honor that work best by offering the same thoughtfulness back again. In what follows, I sketch a response to *Weeps* that looks at its position on five topics—faith, satisfaction, premortality, evolution, and agency—and offer, in return, a mix of sincere amens and honest disagreements.

1. Practicing Faith

In its first chapter, *Weeps* argues that faith is a response to uncertainty. Only our uncertainty about God can make our decision to be faithful meaningful because "an overwhelming preponderance of evidence on either side would make our choice as meaningless as would a loaded gun pointed at our heads."[1] Faith like this has its place, but I doubt that this kind of uncertainty is ordinary. For instance, in this same chapter, *Weeps* describes the death of a friend who had a faith that "did not seem a choice for her. It descended upon her as naturally and irresistibly as the heavy snow that fell on her upstate New York farm."[2] If this friend's belief in God was natural and irresistible, is her faith still meaningful?

It seems to me that the most salient feature of belief is often its involuntary character. Our beliefs are generally given as common sense conclusions that are drawn from a shared but unchosen background of practices, institutions, and assumptions. Depending on the infrastructures we inhabit, God's existence may or may not show up as a common sense conclusion. But, in either case, it is a conclusion that is unlikely to be freely chosen.

What then of faith? When slipping from one existential framework to another, we may experience a dark night of the soul. But such dark nights of uncertainty are typically brief and faith is necessary even (and perhaps especially) when we are *not* in crisis and our place in a framework is firmly settled. In most situations, faith is not a choice about *what* to believe but a choice about *how* we respond to beliefs we did not choose.

Faith is not the same thing as belief or common sense. For some, belief in God comes easily and naturally. Belief isn't a choice and can't be unchosen. God, like words or air, just is. But this isn't enough. Though this common sense belief in God's reality can be a blessing, it can also be a hurdle to practicing faith. It can lull us into thinking that the hard work of being faithful is done when, in fact, we haven't even started. On the other hand, for some, God's absence is itself an obvious aspect of the world as its given. God's improbability presents itself as a fact not as a choice. And while this kind of common sense godlessness can obviously be a barrier, it's not the end of the story. It too can open a path to God by freeing you from common sense idolatries. Neither kind of common sense is faith. Whether God is or isn't obvious to us, the work is the same. Faith is a willingness to lose our souls in faithfully caring

---

1. Terryl Givens and Fiona Givens, *The God Who Weeps: How Mormonism Makes Sense of Life* (Salt Lake City: Ensign Peak, 2012), 4.
2. Ibid., 3.

for the work that's been given to us. Common sense theist, common sense atheist, common sense (or anguished!) agnostic—the work is the same. Each must practice faith. Each must choose to care rather than wish or run.[3]

Weeps claims that "the greatest act of self-revelation occurs when we *choose* what we will believe, in that space of freedom that exists between knowing that a thing is, and knowing that a thing is not."[4] I'm hesitant to agree. It seems to me that the greatest act of revelation comes when we faithfully care for what God, unchosen, has given. Faith, on this account, is still a choice, but it's a choice of a different kind.

2. Saving Satisfaction

Weeps argues that the world is inadequate to satisfy our desires. "Who has never felt the utter inadequacy of the world to satisfy the spiritual longings of our nature?"[5] It is clearly true that the world is inadequate to our desires and that, in the end, it cannot satisfy our "insatiable longing for wholeness."[6] But *Weeps* goes on to claim that the world's inability to satisfy our desires compels us to posit the existence of an object that *could* satisfy them: namely, God. This is a classic theological move with a prestigious pedigree: our longing for wholeness and completion is strong evidence that *something* must exist that *can* make us whole.

Weeps invokes this pedigree by way of both Aristophanes and Augustine. To dramatize our longing and brokenness, Plato's Aristophanes tells a story about how human beings originally had four legs, four arms, and two heads. But, full of ourselves, we angered the gods and Zeus split us in two as punishment, condemning us to wander the earth as half-persons with just one head, two arms, and two legs. As a result, humans are hungry for sex because it allows us—at least temporarily—to put ourselves back together. Of this, *Weeps* says:

> Aristophanes was surely half-joking, but he captures brilliantly our sense of incompleteness and longing for wholeness, for intimate

---

3. Compare, here, my chapter on "Faith" in Adam S. Miller, *Letters to a Young Mormon* (Provo, Utah: Maxwell Institute, 2013), 25–30.

4. Givens and Givens, *God Who Weeps*, 5.

5. Ibid., 40.

6. Ibid., 41.

union with another human being who fits us like our other half. Yet even when we find true love and companionship in the rediscovered other, the restoration that should fulfill us falls short; Aristophanes himself is baffled. It is as if, coming together, we are haunted by the memory of an even more perfect past, when we were even more whole and complete, and this suspicion lends an indefinable melancholy to our present lives. . . . So what can we make of this unsatisfied longing, this sense of a primordial loss that no human love can heal?[7]

The Christian tradition, Augustine in particular, picks up on this same longing and says: "Aha! You feel this way because *God* is your one true other half!" But, as *Weeps* asks, what *should* we make of this unsatisfied longing? Are hungers that will not quit an accidental defect of sin and mortality? Or is this hunger an inseparable feature of what it means to be alive and, perhaps especially, alive in Christ?

I won't deny that it is possible for our restless hearts to find rest in God, but I do want to deny that this rest results from the *satisfaction* of our desires. God does not save us from our hungers by satisfying them. God saves us from the tyranny of our desires by saving us from the impossible work *of* satisfying them. God may be what we desire, but God's arrival does not quench this desire. It gives it. And in giving it, God means to show us how living life depends on caring for rather than being done with desire. Rather than trying to simply satisfy desire, we must be faithful to life by being faithful to the unquenchable persistence of the desires that animate us as alive. Life depends on our being open and incomplete. To be "whole" is to be dead. The heavens are filled with an unquenchable fire. Only hellfire dies down. Jesus liberates us from the problem of desire by saving our desires rather than solving them.

3. Weighing Preexistence

Weeps argues that our world can't support its own weight. Life, meaning, agency, and morality aren't native stock but must be imported from elsewhere. Meaning and stability are drawn from off-world accounts. Here, our doctrine of a premortality is a handy answer as to why things still manage to make sense when our world is so senseless. "The only basis for human freedom and human accountability is a hu-

---

7. Ibid., 13.

man soul that existed before birth as it will after death. Moral freedom demands preexistence, and preexistence explains human freedom."[8] Because this world is too weak, "there must be a true beginning rooted in a time and place of greater dignity and moment."[9] This kind of theological outsourcing is, again, a classic gesture with a prestigious pedigree.

The issue is *identity*. Given how messy and multiple the world is—and this includes, especially, our split and messy selves—there must be (the story goes) some deeper source of unity and identity. Against the complicated dependencies of this world, there must be "an independent, existing principle of intelligence within us."[10] Moreover, "a sense of unease in the world and the poignant yearnings and shadowy intimations of an eternal past, attest to a timeless heritage at the core of human identity."[11] To be spiritually solvent, we need an "identity that lies deeper than our body, rooted beyond actions, reaching past memory."[12] The only trouble with this approach is its nihilism.

You must, of course, decide for yourself, but I endorse Nietzsche's sharp critique of our Christian tendency to devalue the present world by anchoring it's true meaning and substance in another. The irony, in this respect, is that *Weeps* is well aware of the Nietzschean critique and it, too, wants to *agree* with Nietzsche: "Nietzsche was right when he said Christians had a tendency to turn away from this life in contempt, to dream of other-worldly delights rather than resolve this-worldly problems."[13] But a sensitivity to this Nietzschean problem never shows up in any of the book's many celebrations of our doctrine of a pre-world as an essential supplement to this world's poverty.

Rather, with respect to preexistence, *Weeps* ignores the Nietzschean critique of theological outsourcing by ignoring the more fundamental Nietzschean critique of identity. Premortality figures large in the book as a ready-made way to stabilize meaning and identity. In this world you may be composed of split and compromised selves that require your patience and care, but beneath this jumble lies a pre-self, a divine self, that doesn't have these same problems. The pre-self is the true, ideal

---

8. Ibid., 51.
9. Ibid., 45.
10. Ibid., 12.
11. Ibid., 6.
12. Ibid., 43.
13. Ibid., 111.

self. Religion is the work of being faithful to this primordial intuition that my self is something better, simpler, and more independent than it appears.

When we hear an echo of this other self, when we intuit that we must be something more ideal than we appear, what are we gesturing toward? "Who is this 'I' we are referring to in such instances? It could just be an idealized self we have in mind, except the sense is too strong that it is our actions that are unreal, not the self to which we compare them. So, is the most plausible candidate for that 'I' really a hypothetical self we might someday be, or is it what the minister and novelist George MacDonald called an 'old soul,' a self with a long history, that provides the contrast with present patterns of behavior?"[14]

This is where *Weeps* and I part ways. Where *Weeps* sees a solution, I see a problem. Where *Weeps* reads this ideal pre-self as what's real and our present split selves as pale shadows, I regard the ideal pre-self as a dubious and sticky fiction and the present, competing, and multiple selves that compose my soul as the truth about what's really eternal. Now, this is not to deny that I have a pre-self from a premortal life. But it is to deny that we should understand this pre-self as something more true, more divine, and more ideal than our present fleshy one. We're not less true and real in this world. We are more true and real here.

On my account, the Mormon doctrine of preexistence is crucial because it *prevents* us from positing a "deeper" and "truer" original self. Preexistence shouldn't be read as a guarantee of my eternal identity and self-possession. It should be read as what guarantees their impossibility. Preexistence names my always preexisting lack of self-possession. It testifies that I have *always already* been emptied into a world that both composes and divides me with its competing loves and demands. Here, both the pre-world and the post-world must be understood as continuous with the messy work of the present one.

Weeps wisely notes that, with respect to the post-world, "it is in the continuity of our lives now with our lives hereafter that we find rescue from the dangerous heaven of fairy tales."[15] I agree. But I would warn that our lives heretofore must also, just as surely, be rescued from such dangerous heavens and fairy tales. Our belief in a preexistence should commit us to the doctrine that our work in this world is the only kind

---

14. Ibid., 44.
15. Ibid., 111.

of work there has ever been: we must work loose from our fantasies of self-identity for the sake of love.

4. Defending Darwin

I'm glad to see that *Weeps* makes room for Darwin, but I wish it had made more. Theologically, Darwin is a sticky widget. On this front, the fact of biological evolution can be approached in one of three ways: (1) we can shut the evolutionary door and pretend we're not home, (2) we can allow it occasional, supervised visits and hope it doesn't make too big a mess, or (3) we can allow that *we* are visitors in the house that it built.

Weeps accommodates something like the second position. And, to the extent that it does, this is a big and welcome step forward in mainstream Mormon discourse. But I'd like to see us take one step more. I'd like to see us explore—carefully and charitably and experimentally—what it might mean for Mormons to see evolution not just as a local twist in God's top-down management of a wholly rational real, but as indicative of a fundamental truth about the contingent world to which both we and God find ourselves given. *Weeps* seems willing to answer the door but (like any wise investigator) it doesn't want to let the discussion move much beyond the doorstep. The following passage is representative:

> Darwin explained how random, incremental change over millions of years, leads to many species developing from one original source, and he proposed mechanisms and processes by which the giraffe acquired his long neck, and our species the miraculous human eye.... In sum, he made it intellectually respectable to be an atheist. Why, then, do we need faith in God and things eternal? Perhaps because the development of complex human beings, with self-awareness and lives filled with love and tears and laughter, is one too many a miracle to accept as a purely natural phenomenon. Perhaps because the idea of God is a more reasonable hypothesis than the endless stream of coincidences essential to our origin and existence here on earth.[16]

Darwin gets a nod, here, but really only to juxtapose the weak contingency of evolutionary processes with the reassuring rationality of a strong theism. While I think this seriously underestimates the explanatory force of these "natural" processes, I also think that *Weeps* is express-

---

16. Ibid., 10–11.

ing a solid, acceptable, mainstream theological response to evolution: evolution *can* be taken seriously as a creative process but *only* insofar as it is an instrument in the hands of a guiding intelligence. Otherwise, evolution involves one "miracle" too many.

This same sentiment is on display in a later passage that chides Darwin for his inability to account for something as powerful and gratuitous as the beauty of the natural world:

> Darwin was sure that even those spectacles of nature that overwhelm us by their beauty, from the peacock's tail to the fragrance of an English rose, serve not man's purposes but their own, which is survival and reproducibility. If anything in nature could be found that had been "created for beauty in the eyes of man" rather than the good of its possessor, it would be "absolutely fatal" to his theory. In other words, maple leaves in autumn do not suddenly transform into stained glass pendants, illuminated by a setting sun, in order to satisfy a human longing for beauty. Their scarlet, ochre, and golden colors emerge as chlorophyll production shuts down, in preparation for sacrificing the leaves that are vulnerable to winter cold, and ensuring the survival of the tree. But the tree survives, *while* our vision is ravished. The peacock's display attracts a hen, *and* it nourishes the human eye. The flower's fragrance entices the pollinator, *but it also* intoxicates the gardener. In that "while," in that "and," in that "but it also," we find the giftedness of life.[17]

I really like this passage. In fact, it is one of my favorites in the book. It is a pitch perfect description of giftedness or grace. But the passage seems to me to offer a stunning account of exactly how evolution *does* work, not a rebuttal that is "absolutely fatal" to its credibility. Evolution works by way of exaptation. The fundamental process is one in which gratuitous features are purposelessly generated *and then these features get repurposed by extant systems for some other productive end.* The "while" and the "and" and the "but it also" fit perfectly with a Darwinian picture. In fact, they epitomize how natural selection works. But what does this mean? What does it mean if something *Weeps* sees as key to defending the *gospel* ends up also being key to defending *evolution* itself?

Generations of theologians are jealous of our day. On no merit of our own, we've inherited the task of probing the theological implications of the planet-sized shift in our self-understanding imposed by the

---

17. Ibid., 36.

latter-day revelations of biological evolution and deep geological time. We have a lot of work to do.

5. Distributing Agency

Weeps takes a hard, all-or-nothing line on agency. It argues that "something is free only if it is not caused or created by something else."[18] Freedom equals freedom from outside influence. The confused and cross-pollinated conditions of mortality compromise free will. Here, there are too many competing claims. "In our present, earthly form, we are clearly the product of forces outside our control that influence our personality, inform our character, and shape our wants and desires. And yet, we know we are free. How can this be, unless there is something at the heart of our identity that was *not* shaped by environment, *not* inherited from our parents, and *not* even created by God?"[19] If we are free, then there must be some part of us that is not conditioned by our earthly conditions.

According to *Weeps,* any freedom that is *given* is, by definition, unfree. Freedom cannot be given or enabled or inherited or created. A doctrine of co-eternality figures large here as the answer to how we're free. If we are free, it must be because we are uncreated, our agency always already given only by ourselves to ourselves. Our ability to act must not be acted upon. Freedom is a form of self-possessed, self-informed, self-determining autonomy.

Along these lines, it follows that we are free in this world only if we freely chose this world. *Weeps* asks: "If we were simply cast adrift on the shore of this strange world, where is the freedom in that?"[20] But, "if we were involved in the deliberations that culminated in creating and peopling this world, then we are not passive victims of providence. We would have entered into conditions of this mortal state aware of the harrowing hazards mortality entails."[21]

I find this account of agency unconvincing. More, I think it obscures the truth about the kind of thing agency is. Take, for instance, the claim that our freedom in this conditioned world depends on our

18. Ibid., 48.
19. Ibid., 50.
20. Ibid., 52.
21. Ibid., 53.

having freely chosen those same conditions in a former life. Does this same logic apply to the preexistence itself? For *Weeps,* if we were also free in the preexistence, then wouldn't it have to be the case that either (1) the preexistence did not, itself, impose any unchosen conditions, or (2) we must have freely chosen even those preexistent conditions in a *pre*-preexistence? Option one seems to me to make little sense of the preexistence, but option two doesn't seem much better. With option two we've just pushed the problem back a level and, to be fair, we'd have to pose the same two alternatives again. And again. Until we reached that ur-moment when we *didn't* find ourselves *already* pitched into a world we didn't choose, conditioned by conditions we didn't will.

This hiccup in the book's treatment of agency isn't decisive, but it is, I think, symptomatic. I'm inclined to think that our doctrine of co-eternality means just the opposite of what *Weeps* proposes. Rather than safely positioning us (and God) beyond the reach of any unchosen conditions, co-eternality guarantees that there is no such unconditioned place. Co-eternality guarantees that the only thing unconditional is the unconditional imposition of always already existing and unchosen conditions. In fact, I'm inclined to think that this is, at root, the reason why it makes sense for us to claim, as *Weeps* surely does, that our Mormon God weeps.

Does this rule out real agency? No. Just the opposite. Unchosen conditions are the condition of possibility for any meaningful agency. The limits that constrain agency enable it. Recall our other Mormon narrative (one that *Weeps* also draws on) about why mortality is so important. Mortality makes agency meaningful because it *limits* our knowledge and *constrains* our agency. "We need the continuing spiritual friction of difficulty, opposition, and hardship, or we will suffer the same stasis as the bee."[22] Friction is the thing. I'm empowered to act by the unchosen and uncontrollable frictions that compose me and oppose me. Agency isn't simple and internal, it's complex and distributed. Agency is niche-dependent. It is a situated gift dependent on context. Agency isn't a kind of autonomy, but a peculiar, reflexive, and responsible kind of heteronomy. My freedom is *always* given and enabled by something other than myself (cf. 2 Ne. 2:26–27).

Agency isn't possessed, then, but borrowed. It isn't a freedom *from* the conditioned world but a freedom *for* that world. Our ability to act is

22. Ibid., 62.

always both empowered and reciprocally affected by that which it acts upon. All active agents are enabled only by their passivity. "Free" agency is a myth. Freedom is never free. Agency always comes at a cost. And that cost is often paid by others. This is why charity is the greatest virtue.

Weeps concedes that, as a matter of fact, agency works this way. Given our mortal conditions, "hardly ever, then, is a choice made with perfect, uncompromised freedom of the will."[23] But I would raise the stakes and push this one step farther: *never*, then, is a choice made with perfect, uncompromised freedom of will. Why? Because a perfect, uncompromised freedom of will is antithetical to the expression of real agency.

My very favorite passage in all of *The God Who Weeps* has to do with the intersection of agency and atonement. *Weeps* wants to know how the atonement can intervene in our lives without ruining the law of agency. The passage asks:

> The question, however, remains: on what basis can the consequences of our choices be deferred or abated? The law of moral agency, of choice and consequence, does not require that we entirely bear the burden of our own choices made in this life because those choices are always made under circumstances that are less than perfect. Our accountability is thus always partial, incomplete. Into that gap between choice and accountability, the Lord steps.[24]

Into that gap between choice and accountability, the Lord steps. That gap, that beat of "imperfection," is what makes room for love. Love is possible because our choices are *always* made under circumstances that are less than "perfect."

Weeps qualifies that "always" with an "in this life," but I don't think that qualification is necessary. The borrowed and incomplete character of our agency is not an "imperfection" in the expression of that agency, but its condition of possibility. And, moreover, it is the condition of possibility for the fullest possible expression of agency: redeeming love. "The paradox of Christ's saving sway is that it operates on the basis of what the world would call weakness."[25] The paradox of agency is the same.

---

23. Ibid., 100.
24. Ibid., 91–92.
25. Ibid., 29.

Chapter 6

A Radical Mormon Materialism: Reading *Wrestling the Angel*

Terryl Givens's *Wrestling the Angel: The Foundations of Mormon Thought: Cosmos, God, Humanity* is a well researched, clearly written, and important book. It is required reading. However, while Givens's account of our received Mormon ideas is generally accurate, his account also highlights some of the theological knots endemic to the tradition. These problem spots cluster, in particular, around Mormonism's commitment to a radical and thoroughgoing metaphysical materialism. As a tradition, we claim to be materialists but we have no working definition of what it means to be materialists, and we continue to uncritically import traditional Christian paradigms that explicitly depend on various forms of idealism. The resulting inconsistencies bear, minimally, serious investigation. In what follows, I will roughly sketch one approach to a radical Mormon materialism and, then, take Givens's treatment of atonement in *Wrestling the Angel* as symptomatic of the kind of theological knots that we, as a tradition, may yet need to thoughtfully untie.

1. Radical Materialism, Latent Idealism

Wrestling the Angel is an important book because (1) it works to give an overview of Mormon thinking on a range of key theological issues, and (2) it situates these Mormon ideas in the broader historical context of Christian thought. Both contributions are valuable.

With these two goals in mind, Givens rightly emphasizes throughout the book that the key Mormon innovation—the innovation that fundamentally reframes a Mormon version of Christianity—is Mormonism's commitment to materialism. In Mormonism, Givens says, "dualism is rewritten as two-tiered monism (spirit as more refined matter), and laws are themselves as eternal as God."[1] Thus, we get from Joseph Smith a "radical materialism" and this "fundamental claim of a thoroughgoing materialism gave indelible definition to the Mormon theological landscape."[2] I think that Givens is right about this and his book does an excellent job of driving home exactly why this is right. As a result, it is my view that one of our theological priorities as contemporary Mormon thinkers should be to think all the way through—as far as we're able—the philosophical and theological ramifications of this radical materialism.

However, on this front, we have a long way to go. Givens illustrates part of our basic problem in the passage cited above: "Dualism is rewritten as two-tiered monism (spirit as more refined matter), and laws are themselves as eternal as God." Though we claim to be radical materialists, it's hard for us to even finish that sentence before a traditional idealism threatens to sneak back into the picture. Givens isn't alone, here. The problem is nearly universal. Refusing to be dualists—that is, refusing to divide the world into the ideal vs. the material—Mormons instead read spirit itself as a kind of matter. But this material monism is then immediately paired with a second claim about the nature of the *laws* governing this materiality.

What about these laws? What is their status? Are they, according to Givens, also material? We are told that these laws are universal, independent of God, and eternally existent. The implied model for these ideal laws is a Pratt-inflected, nineteenth-century brand of Newtonian physics, but I don't think the details are especially important. It wouldn't matter if we were to instead read the laws as Platonic or transcendental rather than Newtonian. In any of these cases, these eternal laws seem to be *ideal*. It's true that, consistent with a radical materialism, Mormonism's God now gets to be material. God the Father gets a body. Even spirits get to be material. But the philosophical vacuum created by God's materiality, by his loss of immaterial ideality, is immediately filled by the ideality of these eternal laws. We've moved some pieces around, but idealism's basic structure remains intact. All the work traditionally

1. Terryl Givens, *Wrestling the Angel: The Foundations of Mormon Thought: Cosmos, God, Humanity* (New York: Oxford University Press, 2015), 43.
2. Ibid., 61.

done by God's own ideal immateriality is now being done by the ideal-ity of these immaterial laws.

2. A Working Definition of Materialism

So what *would* a radical and thoroughgoing materialism look like? Traditionally, the whole of the Western philosophical tradition is in ba-sic agreement about a handful of intertwined features that distinguish what is material from what is ideal. Plato himself hammers home these features in dialogue after dialogue, perhaps most famously in *The Re-public*. We shouldn't accept these traditional definitions uncritically, but it would be idiosyncratic to start someplace else.

Classically, we have access to what is material by way of our five bodily senses, and these senses receive information about things that are (1) particular, (2) composite, and (3) subject to change. On the oth-er hand, we have access to what is ideal by way of the mind, and the mind receives information about things that are (1) general, (2) simple, and (3) unchanging. The body receives information about things that are particular, composite, and subject to change because our bodies are themselves particular, composite, and subject to change. The mind (or soul) receives information about things that are general, simple, and unchanging because the mind is itself general, simple, and unchanging. Like knows like. We see, here, the grounds for the traditional Western definition of the soul as immaterial: if the soul weren't itself ideal, im-material, and eternal, it would be impossible for us to know ideal, im-material, and eternal things.

More, these complementary triads that define both the material and ideal are composed of tightly interlocking parts. Material things are subject to change and dissolution because they are composed of more than one part: composed of parts, they can be rearranged and fall apart. Also, it is because material things are composed of parts that they are themselves localized and particular (i.e., part-icular). Similarly, ideal things are eternal because they are simple: they can't be rearranged or fall apart because they have not parts. And, having no parts, they must also be general rather than particular. All of this is Western philosophy 101.

For the moment, let's take these traditional definitions as a starting point. Let's assume, as Givens does, that Mormonism is committed to a monistic materialism. This materialism can be "two-tiered" and allow for the existence of spirit, ideas, and laws, but all such things would still themselves have to be fundamentally material. Otherwise, we're back to either a dualism or a metaphysical idealism rather than a monistic materialism. Minimally, then, a thoroughgoing materialism would commit us to the claim that reality is fundamentally: (1) particular, and (2) plural.[3] For simplicity's sake, let's leave aside, for the moment, the related issue of change.[4]

What, then, are the implications of this materiality? Does this commitment to materiality mean that Mormons don't believe in spirit? No, as Givens has already pointed out it just means that Mormons claim that spirit is itself material. That is, it means that spirit is itself both particular and plural. Does this commitment to materiality mean that Mormons don't believe that ideas, generalities, and abstractions are real? Again, no. Ideas are definitely real. It just means that ideas and abstractions are themselves material. That is, ideas and abstractions are themselves particular and plural. The same follows for general laws. Given our thoroughgoing materialism, laws can certainly be real, but if they want to exist, they have to be material and, more, if they want to be material, they have to be particular and plural.

This is the key. Though ideas may map (by way of abstraction) some set of relations among the networks of material things that constitute our worlds, these abstractions do *not* escape the plane of par-

---

3. Now, granted, this definition of materialism is naïve in some respects. To be rigorous I think that we would need to drop the compromised language of "particularity" and deploy, instead, the kind of logics that evade traditional part/whole dialectics altogether—the kind of logics explored by thinkers like Giorgio Agamben, Alain Badiou, François Laruelle, Bruno Latour, and others. However, without dragging logics of exception, set theoretical approaches, or non-standard quantum philosophy into the mix, I think we can cover a lot of initial ground with just the traditional model. For those interested in the details involved in rethinking religious ideas in the context of a radical materialism, this is my area of professional expertise. See either of my monographs on the topic: *Badiou, Marion and St Paul: Immanent Grace* (London: Continuum, 2008) or *Speculative Grace: Bruno Latour and Object-Oriented Theology* (New York: Fordham University Press, 2013).

4. Though, for what it's worth, I think a radical and thoroughgoing materialism would also commit Mormonism to a radical and thoroughgoing dynamism. If, then, the costs of such a materialism start to seem too high, this may be an indication that Mormonism is *not* actually committed to a radically monistic materialism. In many respects, this is likely the simplest response to most of the issues raised in this essay.

ticular material things to hover over or govern that plane. Rather, such idealizations are themselves *one more* material thing *added* to those networks of material things.

This point can be hard to grasp at first. Consider, by way of example, a paper road map. Road maps are useful because they abstract and condense a certain profile from the material network of roads that they represent. The map, as map, doesn't care at all about the concrete or paint these roads are made of (it leaves these real features entirely aside). The map just cares instead about the stable but relative position of each road in relation to all the other roads and then it uses ink and paper to reproduce those relations on a dramatically miniaturized scale. However—and this is the point—though this map is a real and at least partially faithful abstraction, it is still itself *one more material thing* in the world, a world that it can only ever *partially* represent. In this case, one could even imagine finding this particular road map, wet from rain, ironically plastered to the surface of one of the particular roads represented on the map itself! *That* is materialism.

The most immediately compelling consequence of treating abstractions and idealities as material things is the following: It is, by definition, impossible for any material network to completely coincide with any idealization (descriptive or normative) of that particular material network. The overlap between the abstraction and the network can only ever be partial because both the network and the abstraction are *themselves* particular things. In other words, the relationship between every idea and every material network that such ideas claim to abstract (or represent or govern) will be structured by an exception that both puts the two into relationship *and* prevents their complete coincidence. Some elements of the network will always be excepted from any given abstraction because the very act of abstraction, as a material process, requires that some profile be foregrounded while other elements are excluded.

But, we might ask, couldn't there still be a *master* abstraction, maybe a set of ideas or laws that captures and governs everything, without exception? Sure, there could be—in an idealism. But not in a radical materialism, not if all "master" abstractions are themselves material and particular and plural. For my part, I don't see any way around this conclusion: any kind of radical and thoroughgoing materialism will necessarily be structured by a generalized state of ontological exceptionalism.

3. Law, Atonement, Materiality

So why does this matter? Allow me to give just one example of where this might matter quite a bit: Givens's explication of atonement in *Wrestling the Angel*'s chapter on salvation. In this chapter, Givens offers an explication of atonement that, while clearly consonant with aspects of the Mormon tradition and elements of Mormon scripture, is also representative of the tensions and inconsistencies endemic to that broader tradition.

What are the implications of a radical materialism for how we think about the nature of atonement? The implication of a Mormon materialism for atonement is just this: *Our materialism rules out the possibility of thinking about atonement as the perfect conformity of particular material individuals with the governing ideality of eternal laws.* Why? Because if these laws are themselves material things that belong to the same plane of materiality as the particular material individuals that they govern, then these laws are themselves particulars, not immaterial universals. Because both humans and the laws are material, their relationship is structured by an exception that both makes possible their overlap and prevents their perfect coincidence.

But this is the problem. Givens's account of the atonement depends on the existence of immaterial universals. It openly depends on a classical dualism. Givens emphatically frames the atonement as the eventually perfect coincidence of material subjects with an ideal law:

> Christ's atonement sets up the conditions for humans to demonstrate through ever better and wiser choices, made in accordance with ever nobler and purer desires, that it is their will to live in a way consistent with the eternal principles Christ modeled throughout his exemplary life. Repentance is therefore an ongoing process of repudiating unrighteous choices, acknowledging Christ's role in suffering the consequences of those sins on our behalf, and our choosing afresh to better effect. The process continues—perhaps eons into the future—*until in perfect harmony humans have reached a sanctified condition that permits perfect atonement with God.*[5]

Or, again: "For Mormons, being made a saint, or sanctification, is a process of aligning the self with eternal principles."[6] Or perhaps most

---

5. Ibid., 235; emphasis mine.
6. Ibid., 238.

clearly: "Salvation is a natural consequence of compliance with law, just as God's own standing is the natural and inevitable consequence of his compliance with law—*which eventual compliance is made possible by the gift of Christ's atonement.*"[7]

For Givens, salvation is defined in terms of alignment and compliance. But if the defining condition of materialism is a thoroughgoing particularism that structures every relationship (especially laws, abstractions, and representations) with an exception, then such alignment is impossible. The misalignment—or only ever partial alignment—of material subjects with material laws is a structural feature of the real, not a local defect of a subject's will (though our wills may still have plenty of local defects).

Givens, I think, is free to disagree with the conclusions that I've just drawn. But, if so, it seems to me that he will have to respond in one of three ways. He'll need to: (1) propose his own definition of materialism that does not hinge on the classically agreed upon characteristics of a material thing's being particular, composite, and temporal—dismissing out of hand this working definition, especially given its well established pedigree, is not enough; (2) propose an alternate reading of his theory of atonement that avoids positing the existence of ideal laws free from the constraints of their materiality (i.e., their particularity); or (3) propose that Mormonism is not actually committed to a radical, thoroughgoing materialism but, instead, has room for a modified form of dualism that allows for the existence of general, immaterial, and eternal laws free from the constraints of materiality.

However, in my opinion, what we need, instead, is a theory of grace that explicates salvation not in terms of the coincidence of a material subject with an ideal law *but in terms of the exception itself.* I can't begin to lay out in this essay what it means to think about salvation itself in terms of an exception, though I have written about it at great length elsewhere.[8] But, more, we are, I think, already familiar with the broad outlines of such a theory because thinking about salvation in terms of an exception—rather than in terms of that exception's elimination—is just what Christianity itself does, most clearly in the writings of Paul.

In this sense, I would argue that Paul's epistle to the Romans is the key to a genuinely radical and thoroughgoing Mormon material-

---

7. Ibid., 238; emphasis original.
8. See, for instance, the first essay in this volume, "A General Theory of Grace."

ism. As Paul demonstrates, salvation is possible, but it is not possible by way of the law. It is impossible to fulfill the law by way of obedience to the law. Only grace can fulfill the law. As a result, it seems to me that, if Mormonism wants to be a materialism, it's going to have to first learn how to be Pauline.

Chapter 7

Reflections on President Uchtdorf's "The Gift of Grace"

President Dieter F. Uchtdorf's April 2015 General Conference talk, "The Gift of Grace," offers a long needed corrective to our Mormon tendency to read the gospel as a kind of secular manual for can-do humanism and self-improvement. It brings our popular thinking more closely in line with what the Bible and, especially, the Book of Mormon teach about grace. But what President Uchtdorf outlines in that Sunday morning talk is what I would call a "special theory" of grace. It addresses just a special, local subset of grace: grace as it is operative in our redemption.

Speaking of grace, President Uchtdorf begins where we usually do, with the problem of sin. As sinners, we are all lost. We have all gone astray, and we cannot save ourselves. We cannot put right what went wrong, and we cannot empower ourselves to become what God intends us to be. "We cannot earn our way into heaven; the demands of justice stand as a barrier, which we are powerless to overcome on our own."[1] More, President Uchtdorf argues that, as a response to the problem of sin, grace must not be understood as a backup plan for our own works. In the talk's most striking and memorable line—a line that deserves to be emblazoned on a legion of t-shirts and needlework samplers—President Uchtdorf claims that "salvation cannot be bought with the currency of obedience; it is purchased by the blood of the Son of God."[2] Why can't salvation be bought with the currency of obedience? Because righteous works only become righteous when they are motivated by the pure love

---

1. Dieter F. Uchtdorf, "The Gift of Grace," LDS General Conference, April 2015, available at https://www.lds.org/general-conference/2015/04/the-gift-of-grace.
2. Ibid.

of Christ. Works only become righteous when they are the *product* of God's grace as that grace works its way out into the world through our hearts and hands. We receive grace by becoming vessels for it.

All of this is good. The problem, though, is that this approach still implicitly frames grace as a response to sin. It corrects our tendency to see grace as a secondary element that comes into play only after we've done what we can to save ourselves, but it leaves sin in the driver's seat.

It's true, of course, that grace *is* God's response to sin. And it is crucial to understand this. But a "special theory" of grace is incomplete because it doesn't go far enough. It leaves intact the impression that God's original plan really was for people to bootstrap themselves into righteousness by way of obedience and that then, *when this fails*, God steps in with his grace as the key to our salvation. In other words, it leaves intact the impression that our works were originally primary with respect to our salvation and that, only because of our failure, must grace then step in, become primary, and save us.

As a result, a "special theory" of grace that understands grace only in terms of redemption doesn't correct the problem of a "works-first" gospel so much as it pushes that problem back a level. Here, grace gets understood as God's "plan A" when it comes to fixing sin, but grace risks remaining "plan B" with respect to an original expectation of perfect obedience. Framing grace as "plan A" in response to sin is a welcome first step, but, in my view, what we really need is a "general theory" of grace, a global theory of grace, that situates this special, local theory in a broader context and articulates grace as "plan A," period.

This is to say that we need a richer sense of grace. We need a sense of grace that is grounded not just in God's *redemption* of the world but that is grounded principally in his *creation* of the world. Grace isn't just a name for how God saves us. It's a name for God's global *modus operandi*, and this M.O. is manifest originally and fundamentally in God's work of creation. To understand grace as it's operative in our redemption, we need to understand redemption as just one of the "three pillars" of eternity: creation, fall, atonement. To understand atonement, we need to understand the fall. But to understand the fall, we need to understand creation. To understand God's special, redeeming act of grace, we need to understand our own fall in relationship to God's general and original act of grace: creation.

A "general theory" of grace would account for grace as a fundamental and constitutive feature of reality itself.[3] And, more, it would understand grace not only as constitutive of reality at some point in the past but as an essential and ongoing feature of everything real. Creation, as a general grace, is not a one-time, past-tense event. Rather, creation is a present-tense, ongoing event that is just as surely and just as palpably operative right now as it was five billion years ago. Grace is this massive, ongoing act of divinely organized creation that involves an uncountable host of agents, human and nonhuman, embedded in irreducible webs of stewardship, consecration, sacrifice, and interdependence. "Glory" is one name for God's grace as it continually brews out of these massive, creative networks of divinely enabled agents.

Now, understanding creation as a grace that is freely and continuously given, we are in a position to understand sin. That is, understanding creation, we can understand the fall. What is sin? Sin is our rejection of this original and ongoing grace. Sin is our refusal of some part of creation. It is a refusal of our having to be part of creation. Or, even better, it is a refusal of our own createdness. Sin is our proud and fearful refusal of our dependence on a world that we didn't ask for, can't control, and can't escape.

Redemption doesn't involve injecting grace at the last moment into a sinful situation that previously lacked it. Rather, because sin is our suppression of creation as a grace, redemption proceeds fundamentally as a *recovery* of the grace that's already actively given. Redemption, in a general theory of grace, must be understood as a subset of God's original grace that is principally manifest in his ongoing work of creation.

In this sense, redemption should be understood as just another mode of creation. Redemption, we might say, is *re*-creation. Redemption is about being re-born into this world as the very world that God was trying to give us from the start. Redemption, unlocked by Jesus, returns us to the ongoing work of creation and, as a result, it recreates us. It returns us to the grace we once refused.

Allow me to reframe this in a way that is more immediate and personal. If God's grace is already given, then what is the problem? Why do I feel so far from grace? Why am I so disappointed, frustrated, and angry? I often feel this way because, dependably, I don't *want* what God

---

3. For an example of such an account see Adam S. Miller, *Speculative Grace: Bruno Latour and Object-Oriented Theology* (New York: Fordham University Press, 2013).

is giving. I don't want the kind of world that's on offer. And, quite often, I don't want to be the kind of thing God has given me to be. I actively resist the grace God is giving.

I don't want to be what I am. I don't want to be weak and ordinary and small and dying. I don't want to be less than the dust of the earth. I don't want to discover, as Moses did, that I am nothing. Having seen God's glory, God withdrew and Moses says, "for this cause I know that man is nothing, which thing I never had supposed" (Moses 1:10). I don't want to suppose this. I want to suppose something else altogether. I want to be something special, something different, something powerful, something exceptional.

The debate between grace and works often gets framed as follows. We ask: how will I get the salvation I want? Will I get what I want purely by hard work? Will I get what I want purely by grace? Or will I get what I want by some combination of the two? But these are the wrong questions. This way of framing the debate misses the whole point. It misses the nature of grace. It isn't a question of whether I'll get what I *wanted* either by way of works or by way of grace. It's a question of whether I'll assent to the grace of what I did *not* want to get and to the grace of who I did *not* want to be. Foremost among the things God is trying to give me is, well, me—this body, this mind, this weakness, this hunger, this passing away. Redemption involves my willingness, first, to just be the hungry, weak, failing thing that I already am. Redemption involves my willingness to accept that gift and treat it as a gift. This grace is free but it's certainly not cheap.

Craig Harline gives an excellent description of this kind of redemption in his mission memoir, *Way Below the Angels: The Pretty Clearly Troubled But Not Even Close to Tragic Confessions of a Real Life Mormon Missionary*. Harline is called to serve a mission in Belgium in the 1970s, and he's pretty sure that God has called him to be something special, something extraordinary. He believes with his whole heart that God is going to do a mighty work through him and that, if he can just be obedient enough, if he can just be perfect enough, he and his companion and the whole mission will be transformed. Belgium's baptismal fonts will overflow. But it's not working. No one will listen. He has trouble with the language. He's tired and frozen and bored and disappointed. He has trouble with his companions.

One winter afternoon as the sun prepares to set at an absurdly early hour, Harline is running on empty. It's only lunchtime, but he can't bear the thought of going back out into the cold to knock endlessly on doors that won't open. So, leaving his companion downstairs, he collapses alone, in the bedroom. He prays. He pleads with God to save him from the emptiness that has seized him because this emptiness has sunk into his bones. Recounting the experience, Harline says:

> Maybe this was the sort of emptiness that mystics said you had to feel before you could really feel God—thus that you had to clear out all the clutter inside, including your notions of who you thought God was and how He worked, and only then were you in a state to let real God in. Or maybe the emptiness was all there was, rather than just some sort of lead-up to being filled by God. Maybe the void was it, period. Probably everyone who feels the void feels it differently, but for me struggling on top of the giant awful lumpy mattress for what seemed like forever but was really only the 15 or 20 minutes it took for the last of the sun's rays to go almost completely horizontal, the emptiness wasn't so much filled as reduced to something smaller and smaller and quieter and quieter, until finally it took the form of a totally silent thought/feeling that calmly but overwhelmingly entered the emptiness inside, and it was just this: *just be yourself.* The idea of just being plain old myself, if by that was meant being myself as currently constituted in the form of a still mostly English-speaking me, just sounded so weak, like God was giving up on me as someone who had the potential to become *really* special. If the thought/feeling *Just be yourself* really was coming from God, then it had to be referring to the *yourself* I eventually would become, my *true* still-dormant self, not the *yourself* I was right now. But I was disturbingly getting the distinct feeling from the thought/feeling that oh yes it was trying to tell me something along the disappointing lines of being content with who I was right then. I should just be my own self, not my special self.[4]

This revelation is redemptive. But it is a revelation that arrives with equal parts relief and disappointment. God sees what I am. God gave me to be just what I am. And if I'm ever to be anything else, anything more, that change will have to start with the hard work of receiving the

---

4. Craig Harline, *Way Below the Angels: The Pretty Clearly Troubled But Not Even Close to Tragic Confessions of a Real Life Mormon Missionary* (Grand Rapids: William B. Eerdmans, 2014), 120–21.

gift that has already been given. If I can't receive this present gift, how could I receive whatever gifts come next?

This is disappointing. I am not what I wanted. I'd hoped for something else, I'd hoped to be something else, and so I've been running away. I've been hiding and pretending and planning. I've worked hard to be obedient and put on a good show. I've worked hard at making a good impression and collecting trophies and gold stars. But those trophies and gold stars are no road to salvation. Obedience is not the currency of salvation. These prizes are not the grace that God is trying to give.

The grace that God is trying to give is much more general and much more obvious. It's hidden in plain sight. It's on display right now, in my lungs and beneath my feet and in the earth's hard crust. It's already given. And God is waiting.

Chapter 8

A Manifesto for the Future of Mormon Thinking

1. Fearless Mormon Thinking

This is a manifesto for the future of Mormon thinking. It is not a description. It is not a prediction. It is, rather, an invitation.

In the future, Mormon thinking will be fearless. It will be fearless in the truth. And the only way to hold a truth fearlessly is, as John says, to hold it with perfect love. "There is no fear in love; but perfect love casteth out fear" (1 Jn. 4:18). Only love is fearless. And only the fearless see the truth. If we fail to love, fear will cloud our eyes and skew our judgment.

In order for thinking itself to be fearless, that thinking must be conducted as an act of love. And in order to be conducted as an act of love, we must do as Jesus says: we must love our enemies.

> Ye have heard that it hath been said, Thou shalt love thy neighbour, and hate thine enemy. But I say unto you, Love your enemies, bless them that curse you, do good to them that hate you, and pray for them which despitefully use you, and persecute you; That ye may be the children of your Father which is in heaven: for he maketh his sun to rise on the evil and on the good, and sendeth rain on the just and on the unjust. For if ye love them which love you, what reward have ye? do not even the publicans the same? (Matt. 5:43–46)

Even sinners love those who love them. Even sinners love those who repeat what they want to hear and confirm what they already know. But such love is thoughtless. Those who love the truth and are fearless in it will be marked by their confidence that every truth can be thought again—indeed, must be thought again—from the position of the enemy. Their confidence in this extension of the truth will be rooted in

God's promise that the truth must rise on the evil and the good, it must rain down on both the just and unjust. All truths, in order to be truths, must be thinkable from the position of the enemy. All truths must be thinkable as an act of love for the enemy.

It is, of course, possible to hold truths in a way that fails to be truthful. It is always possible to bear a truth untruthfully, to wield the truth as a weapon against my enemy or as a shield to justify my stupor. And it is, of course, always possible to assume that every truth held by my enemy must be held in just this way, in bad faith, blinkered, untruthfully. But this is a scam. It's a diversion.

The very work of seeing truth as truth, of bearing that truth truthfully, depends on our willingness to take up the perpetually necessary project of thinking through the truth again—always once more—from the position of the enemy. Every truth must be thought through again because truths are bigger than we can manage. They cannot be confined to our own limited perspective. Though truths may fill us and transfigure us, they always do so only from somewhere else and on the way to somewhere new. A truth that is small enough to be thinkable only from my position and only in opposition to my enemy is no truth at all.

To say that a truth must be thinkable from the position of the enemy is not to say that truths are relative to one's perspective. Rather, it is to insist that they are not. It is to say that truths must be capable of traversing and transfiguring every perspective that greets them. Truths, borne truthfully, compel us to acknowledge both their capacity to transfigure every position and the reality that they are, as yet, only partial in their extension. What truths we have, we have only in part—much more is promised. And those truths already entrusted to us have barely begun to fill our *own* hearts and minds, let alone the world.

To think a truth again, this time from the enemy's position, is to engage in the hard work of discovering what happens when we no longer treat the truth as proprietary—as owned by us, proper to us, and relative to our own perspective—and instead pursue its extension beyond our borders to see what happens when the truth also transfigures the position occupied by the enemy. To think a truth again is to investigate both how it can transform the enemy's position and what it looks like once I've let it loose in the world. Granted, my enemy's perspective is too small and too narrow to hold the truth. But, occupied by a truth, that position can be transfigured. This is the promise of truth: transfiguration. Though, on this score, the same thing may be just as truthfully said of my own position. Love's extension of the truth is imperative because I must also grant that my own perspective is too small and too narrow to hold the truth. Whatever tenuous relation I have to the truth can only be preserved if that truth is shared.

In summary, then, the point is straightforward. Thinking that is not fearless is thoughtless. And thinking can only be fearless when it is conducted as an act of love. And thinking can only be conducted as an act of love when it traverses the position occupied by the enemy, transfiguring in the process myself, the truth, and the enemy.

In what follows, I want to explore two examples of fearless thinking conducted as an act of love for the enemy. First, a thinking that transfigures the secular. And second, a thinking that transfigures subjectivity.

2. Transfiguring the Secular

Say we grant the claim that secularism is, today, the enemy of Mormonism. What follows?

What follows is that secularism ought to be first in line for Mormon love and Mormon thinking. Secularism ought to be greeted fearlessly. No one should be thinking harder or better about secularism than Mormonism. And no one should be doing more to rethink truths from the secular position than Mormonism.

Now, again, a fearless extension of the truth to the secular position doesn't amount to either an adoption or a rejection of that position. Rather, the work of thinking must transfigure that position. It must proceed as an occupation that simultaneously transfigures all three elements involved: the enemy, Mormonism, and the truth. If our fearless thinking doesn't transfigure all three, then, whatever else was managed, truth will fail.

More, let me emphasize that love's extension of the truth, its refusal to treat the truth as narrow and proprietary, is not a gesture of appeasement. It is a form of resistance. It is a form of resistance that refuses to allow the enemy to be the enemy, that refuses to allow the enemy to be positioned as what must be excluded or opposed. Animated by love, real thinking is a form of fearless resistance that begins by offering again and again that most counterintuitive (but most Christian) of all gestures: it turns the other cheek. Rather than facing down the enemy, real thinking turns its head to see what the enemy was seeing. This gesture of love embodies the deepest possible act of resistance: it contests the enemy's right to be an enemy rather than a friend.

Secularism needs to be contested. But if it is contested in the wrong way—if it is met with aggression or capitulation—then our resistance risks only reinforcing the oppositions upon which secularism itself depends. For the sake of truth, we must contest the founding oppositions that define secularism as such.

Secularism defines itself in opposition to the not-secular. That is, it defines itself in opposition to religion. To agree to this opposition, to agree that secularism and religion are enemies, is to have agreed in advance that secularism should be allowed to frame the debate. Once this right is granted and its attendant opposition codified, truth has already been compromised. Ceding this opposition allows secularism to define—for both the secular person and the religious person—what religion is and it allows secularism to define itself in opposition. Religion never understood itself as the "not-secular" until secularism defined it that way. And if religion wants to be serious about contesting secularism, it shouldn't start by granting that point. It shouldn't start by ratifying secularism's right to be the enemy. And it definitely shouldn't start, as many seem to do, by taking a secular premise—that religion is, essentially, the not-secular—as the key to understanding religion itself. Transfiguring the secular will require that we steadfastly refuse to grant the premise that religion and secularism are enemies.

You've doubtless seen, on a thousand fronts, how this same sad fight plays out over and over between the secular and the religious under their "liberal" and "conservative" aliases. The liberal and conservative pair is a secular pair. To accept their opposition as a frame for combatively appropriating rather than compassionately extending truths is, again, to have undercut truth right from the start. It doesn't matter, here, that the conservative position is "opposed" to the secular position because the opposition is itself secular. In fact, it's this very opposition that defines the legitimacy of secularism. The resulting irony is pretty thick: loyal conservative opposition to liberal positions may goose some local tactical wins, but the astonishingly fierce loyalty of conservatives to the rules of this *secular* game guarantees, in the end, their strategic defeat.

Fearless Mormon thinking will refuse to play this game. It will refuse to carve up the world into the secular versus the religious (or the liberal versus the conservative), and it will, instead, roam the whole world searching for truths, extending truths, transfiguring truths, and thinking through every manifestation of truth—always once more, always again—wherever those truths happen to show themselves. Fearless Mormon thinking will undermine wholesale the validity of the distinctions upon which the secular project depends and it will construct a new space for thinking that won't allow the secular to operate as religion's governing opposition. Then, having decommissioned secularism as a governing term in religious self-understanding, it will evaluate, absorb, and repurpose the best elements of secularism itself. And, finally, in the process of transfiguring the secular, Mormonism will itself be transfigured by its love for the enemy.

3. Transfiguring Subjectivity

Say we grant that Mormonism is profoundly threatened by the claim that our religion is just in our heads. Say we grant that Mormonism is threatened by the claim that, at best, Mormonism is a subjective pastiche of wishful thinking, soggy reasoning, willful self-deception, DIY clichés, middle management kitsch, and rose-tinted history that, as a whole, not only lacks objective reality but actively suppresses it. What follows? What follows is that fearless Mormon thinking ought to occupy this position. It ought to adopt this critique as God's own truth and find out how much water it can actually hold.

This enemy is too big a threat for fearless Mormon thinking to do anything other than love it with a whole heart. If hiding in the clouds used to be an option, it isn't any more. Fearless Mormon thinking needs to invest in a massively sensitive and systematic investigation of religious subjectivity. It needs to investigate Mormon head-space and see what that head is made of—what thoughts compose it, what affects drive it, what languages articulate it, what neuroses compromise it, what stories organize it.

If you take seriously the possibility that Mormonism boils down to fuzzy feelings and wishful thinking, what will you find? You will discover, first and foremost, something surprising about the nature of the mind, something that you might not have seen at all if you hadn't dared to love this enemy. If you take as a starting point the claim that Mormonism is just in people's heads and then actually investigate—rather than dismiss—what's in those heads, you will find, overwhelmingly, that those heads are full of body. You will find that the head is stuffed full not just with thoughts but with light and color and smells and sounds and tastes and sensations. And if, then, you investigate what's in that body, you will find that the body is itself full of the world. You will find that the world is constantly flooding both the body and the head with ideas and sensations that rush in with sufficient force and impose themselves with sufficient insistence that everything in the head is always, though in complicated ways, woven into the fabric of the world. You will find that mind and world aren't autonomous and that, despite their differences, they have always already bled into each other in a thousand tangled and inseparable ways. You will find that mind and world are composed of common ground. In short, you will find that there is no such thing as "just" the head. That position, once occupied, is transfigured.

This is a basic phenomenological point. It shouldn't come as a surprise. Though, too, it shouldn't come as a surprise that, in itself, this point is no defense against the claim that Mormonism may, like Scientology, have woven itself into the fabric of the world in harmful, misleading, and unjustifiable ways. But still, granting this point is important because, at the very least, it shows how a willingness to love this enemy has already reframed the basic question at hand. The real issue isn't whether the contents of Mormon heads are woven, irrevocably, into the fabric of the world itself. They are. The real question has to do with the strength, character, and value of this weaving.

By reframing the question, we've clarified the nature of the work to be done. Occupying this subjective position, the aim of fearless Mormon thinking must be to investigate with great care and precision the nature of this weaving. Rather than being, fundamentally, in the business of fending off enemies of its otherworldly claims about angels and mummies and miracles, Mormon thinking, steered by its love for this vital enemy, will turn back to the more basic business of investigating the primal ground that head and world share. This primal site where head and world bleed into each other is ground zero for the manifestation of both life and grace. This primal site is the place where religion is lived rather than talked about. To this end, Mormon thinking is called to patiently and fearlessly investigate (1) what our religious claims look like when, shorn for the moment of their transcendence, they occupy just this robustly immediate, available, and often empirical ground, and (2) what happens to this shared ground when it is itself transfigured by that occupation.

Brought so low to the ordinary ground of everyday things, what does Mormonism look like? Can Mormonism breathe the air down there? Can it live? Some things will doubtless look different from this low angle, but I'm confident that Mormonism can breathe the air just fine. You don't need a spacesuit if you're not in outer space. In fact, it seems to me that a fearless investigation of this subjective position, driven as it is by a love for its enemy, may simply coax into the open something that should have already been obvious to those whose hearts and minds are woven into the world by way of Mormonism: the truth that religion is not, fundamentally, about supernatural stuff.

This is not to say that supernatural things aren't real or that your neighbor down the street may not be entertaining angels. But I think it's fair to say that, even if granted, such things are pretty rare and peripheral. I think it's fair to say that they are clearly not what a Sunday service is aiming at. Church isn't magic and prayers aren't incantations. You can sit in church for three hours each Sunday for decades and never see anything supernatural. You can read and pray everyday for a lifetime and never see anything supernatural. You can birth and bless and bury whole generations and never see anything supernatural. Does this mean religion is a sham? That it's broken? That it doesn't work? Or does it mean that something else, in plain sight, is going on instead? God seems to pretty intentionally keep supernatural stuff—including his own supernatural self—off the table for most people most of the time. Why be so coy if supernatural stuff is the point? Why spirit all the direct evidence away? Why so many complications and detours? Why have sermon after apostolic sermon about loving your ordinary neighbor if such ordinary things were a diversion from the real supernatural deal?

In itself, I don't take credulity to be a spiritual virtue. And I take God's palpable reticence on supernatural things to be more a blessing than a curse. His reticence is a gift that saves us from distraction. It brings us back, as God seems to intend, to the earth and the sun and the trees at hand. It keeps our eyes clear and our priorities straight. It keeps life's grip tight.

For my part, I suspect that it may be only from this heretical perspective—from the enemy's perspective, occupied and loved—that the real richness and power and beauty of an ordinary Mormon life can come into sharp focus. I suspect that we may only be able to see what Jesus wants to show us if we manage to love our enemies as Jesus asked. And, more, I suspect that if, in the end, Mormonism can justify its way of weaving together hearts and heads and worlds, it will only be able to do so by digging deep into the already available ground of ordinary Mormon life. Magic rocks and golden plates and stars beyond Kolob—even granted the full force of their objective reality—are far too small and weak to bear a burden of proof that only life itself, in the fullness of its banality and beauty, could ever hope to meet. Helping us to fearlessly acknowledge this may be the enemy's most enduring gift.

Chapter 9

Network Theology:
Is it Possible to be a Christian
but not a Platonist?

1. Introduction

I want to pose a question that, though of obvious interest to Mormons, is ecumenical in spirit and speculative in content. When I say that it is ecumenical in spirit I mean that the hypothesis I propose here, in order to be taken seriously, depends only on (1) a broad, nondenominational commitment to Christianity, and (2) a sensitivity to the limitations of a classical understanding of the world. My speculative, ecumenical question is this: is it possible to be a Christian but not a Platonist?

It is, of course, well documented that Christianity has been explicitly tied to one kind of Platonism or another for a very long time. But my question is not primarily interested in this historical relationship between Christianity and Platonism. Rather, I mean to use the term "Platonist" in a very broad way as a kind of placeholder that collects under one heading every understanding of the world that adheres to the founding principles of classical metaphysics: (1) unity must precede multiplicity, (2) essence has priority over existence, and (3) matter is dependent on form. In the end, these metaphysical principles are simply different ways of making the same classically Platonic point: for Plato, the One subordinates the many.

The obvious difficulty is that this extremely broad characterization of Platonism includes practically everyone, from Parmenides to Aristotle to Descartes to Kant. Whether the One is given priority as a Platonic form, an Aristotelian species, an Epicurean atom, a Cartesian subject, or a Kantian transcendental, unity trumps multiplicity. Further, these Platonic principles are so deeply engrained in a religious understanding of the world that (at least as far as Western religions are concerned) they seem to be constitutive of a religious worldview, period. This is true to the extent that, given my characterization of Platonism, my question about whether it's possible to be a Christian but not a Platonist may initially appear nonsensical.

Let's reverse direction, though, and ask from the opposite side what principles would define a non-Platonic understanding of the world. If one were to be a Christian but not a Platonist, what would one need to hold? We can, I think, summarize a response with the following three principles: (1) reality is originally multiple, (2) unity or (at-one-ment) is an operation, not a given, and (3) all form (or spirit) is matter. My thesis is that we might elaborate the characteristics of this kind of world, a world founded on the priority of matter and multiplicity, through contemporary thinking about complex networks and that network thinking is surprisingly resonant—in a way that Platonism is not—with the core of the Christian message.

2. What is Network Thinking?

Network thinking is defined by its avoidance of the kind of essentialism, emphasis on intentional design, and commitment to primordial unity that mark Platonism. In general, network thinking describes the world as an overlapping set of flat, material systems whose primary traits include the fact they are:

1. Complex. To say that a network is complex is to say that its structure cannot be effectively compressed. A complex network cannot be analytically reduced to its constituent parts or compressed into a simplified form without obscuring the network itself. A complex network is constituted as such by its rich patterns of meaningful but often irregular relationships. The internet is probably the most obvious example of a complex network.

2. Dynamic. Networks are complex, in part, because they are fluid and dynamic. Truly rich and complex patterns emerge in a network because its paths of connection are continually wired, traversed, and re-wired by use or disuse. The human brain is an example of a complex, dynamic network.

3. Open. In order to be dynamic and avoid static patterns, networks must continually "communicate" with other, overlapping networks (these overlapping systems form a given network's environment). And, in order to be in communication with its environment, a network must be open rather than closed. In biological terms, the difference between an open and a closed network is the difference between life and death.

4. Distributed. Complex networks lack a center of gravity or single, unifying anchor point. Rather, their structure is distributed over a space with multiple, overlapping, and localizing network hubs.

5. Looped. The interactions of a complex network are sufficiently rich as to be reflexive. Information and energy can be relayed through a given hub and then return back to that same hub as a modified or amplified message. These feedback loops help account for how very small, local interactions can, within a complex system, produce disproportionately large, architectonic effects.

6. Nonlinear. To say that a complex network is characterized by nonlinearity is to say that in such systems causality is not simply additive. Instead, the network's looped, distributed, and dynamic structure organizes its responses to input around "tipping points" that allow small changes in the system to produce surprisingly large effects. The weather, for instance, is famously difficult to predict precisely because it is a nonlinear system in which small changes in the vicinity of a tipping point (like the temperature at which water freezes) can create huge swings in weather patterns.

7. Self-organizing. Network thinking hinges on its verifiable descriptions of how open, dynamic systems are capable of both adaptation and self-organization. Matter, interacting without design or intention, is capable of producing finely tuned large-scale patterns. Matter—contrary to what has been held by nearly the entire Western philosophical tradition—can organize itself into meaningful and productive forms. And these productive forms are capable of adapting, again without the intervention of design or intention, to changes in their environment. The obvious example, here, is biological evolution.

8. Emergent. Material networks capable of self-organization produce emergent phenomena. Without design or consultation,

large quantities of simple and predetermined local interactions between the parts of a network can cause calibrated macro patterns to spontaneously emerge. This emergent, macro-order is said to be "free" because it can be neither reduced to nor predicted by the local interactions upon which it depends. Think, here, of how ants spontaneously act in synchronized ways or of how, in the course of a week, you might suddenly find all the students in a class wearing the same new kind of shoes. The "invisible hand" of the market is a good example of an emergent phenomenon.

9. Historical. Because they are dynamic and adaptive, complex networks bear with them a history that shapes their present and future responses to input. In one sense, the structure of the network is itself a record of that network's history. Which connections are strong, which links have been forged, which hubs have taken on increasingly important roles—all of this is *contingent* on what interactions the network has transmitted, and all of this shapes how the network will yet respond to future changes in its environment. In order to understand a network, one must know something of its history. There are no ahistorical or atemporal networks.

10. Local. As emergent, distributed, and overlapping, complex networks are neither reducible to their parts nor totalizable into abstract wholes. Complex networks produce unity of various kinds, but they are not One. As a result, network thinking is profoundly sensitive to a system's localization in time and space. Local relationships are a network's beating heart. Languages, for example, are complex networks that constantly produce meaning and unity, but language is decisively sensitive to context and locale.

11. Flat. Even with emergent self-organization, network thinking draws no fundamental, ontological distinctions between the kinds of things there are. A network ontology is fundamentally flat and recognizes everything as essentially material. In a network world, there is no "great chain of being" with its vast hierarchy of rank. Differences between complex systems are differences in scale and organization, not differences in kind. The human body, for example, is a complex system of a certain, familiar scale. But it is also composed of webs of complex

systems (e.g., the nervous system, the respiratory system, etc., which are themselves composed of even smaller systems) while the body is also itself a component of larger complex networks (e.g., families, schools, economies, etc.).

Cast in terms of these eleven network characteristics, a non-Platonic but Christian thinking addresses itself to the world as it is given in the age of democracy, evolution, and globalization: as a complex, dynamic, open, distributed, looped, nonlinear, historical, local, and flat set of overlapping material systems in which order and meaning unaccountably intervene as emergent, self-organizing phenomena.

Now, having rolled through a rough description of how network thinking breaks with Platonism, I want to turn my attention to how a network theology may resonate more profoundly with Christianity's core teachings than Platonism. In order to do so, I will consider four hypothetical questions:

1. What if God is not a king?
2. What if truth is a process, not a product?
3. What if grace is immanent?
4. What if the soul is a network?

3. What if God is not a king?

Metaphysically, Platonism requires a king. For Plato, the world itself depends on a sovereign distance between an original, transcendent One and the multitude. Monarchies and Platonic thinking go hand in hand. Thus, to dispense with Platonic unity in favor of a network's multiplicity is, in a sense, to dispense with the king in favor of a democracy because democracy is a self-organizing network of distributed powers.

In order to be Christians but not Platonists, we would need to hear in Jesus's declaration of the "kingdom of God" more than a hint of subversive irony. We would need to hear him strain, in his exemplification of what it means to be divine, to distance God from our vain assumptions about what it means to be a king. To be a "king," as Jesus points out to his apostles, is to be the servant of all. "Whosoever will be chief among you, let him be your servant: even as the Son of man came not to be ministered unto, but to minister, and to give his life a ransom for many" (Matt. 20:27–28). To say that *this* is the essence of kingship is to have thoroughly redefined the term.

In Christianity, divinity is revealed in kenotic acts of divine self-emptying. No one states this more clearly than Paul in his letter to the Philippians:

> [Jesus], being in the form of God, thought it not robbery to be equal with God: but made himself of no reputation, and took upon him the form of a servant, and was made in the likeness of men: and being found in fashion as a man, he humbled himself, and became obedient unto death, even the death of the cross. Wherefore God also hath highly exalted him, and given him a name which is above every name: that at the name of Jesus every knee should bow ... [and] every tongue should confess that Jesus Christ is Lord, to the glory of God the Father. (Philip. 2:6–11)

Network thinking countermands the temptation to read this passage as a Platonist. A Platonic reading of this passage would read Jesus's humility as a temporary abstinence from real, sovereign power and emphasize his triumphant re-enthronement. A network reading, however, would not split Jesus's servitude from his Lordship. Rather, it would read his humility as a revelation about the abiding truth of God's "kingship." Jesus is not exalted because he temporarily deigns to serve. He is exalted because he reveals humility as the essence of divinity. He reveals the truth of power as solidarity rather than sovereignty.

In this way, network theology gives us room to understand democracy as inherently sacred. Jesus's "kingdom" is such that it proclaims solidarity with the multitude in a move that flattens class and rank (his own included) onto a single horizontal plane, even as it undermines our vain commitment to the vertical, stratified model of a monarchy. Here, power is not delivered from the top-down, but produced from the bottom-up. Rather than being imposed from an atemporal standpoint that transcends the multitude, God's power emerges through the dynamic, local interactions of the network itself.

4. What if truth is an ongoing process, not a static product?

A traditional understanding of truth as the correct correspondence of an internal idea with an external state of affairs depends on a stable, hierarchical background of fixed essences. Traditionally, truth depends on the hard guarantee—be it empirical, transcendent, or transcenden-tal—of some brand of Platonism. But if the world consists of flat, adap-tive, and overlapping networks, then what place is there for truth?

While network thinking must jettison a representational under-standing of truth as a fixed product, it offers instead a description of truth as a specialized network process. As an ongoing process, truth is defined in opposition to knowledge. If knowledge is understood as the publicly agreed upon network of banked "common knowledge" avail-able at any given time, then truths are specialized processes that trace novel paths through the network, revealing inconsistencies and display-ing overlooked constellations of meaning. As ongoing processes, truths are successful to the degree that they are able to overwrite a network's previous self-understanding with one that meshes more finely and pro-ductively with its own unfolding. Knowledge, then, is the residue of a successful truth.

In this sense, truths are always tied to the specific networks of knowledge in which they are actively at work. This, however, does not relativize truths such that the center no longer holds—distributed net-works have no such center to begin with. Rather, network thinking concentrates and localizes the force of every truth we set in motion.

Paul's evangelization of the Christian proclamation models this understanding of truth as a network process. As a truth, the gospel is literally an announcement of good news, a divine proclamation that it is possible to trace new paths through the world's open but fragmented networks. As Paul explains in 1 Corinthians 1:17–31, the new paths forged by Jesus's truth initially appear as "foolishness" in relation to the banked "wisdom of the wise" (vv. 18, 19) because Christianity ignores the world's distribution into Jews and Greeks. The multitude known to the world as foolish, weak, and base—that is to say: as non-beings—are displayed in Christ's redistribution of the world as its productive, living truth (cf. vv. 26–27). Here, the measure of such a truth is not its cor-respondence to how things are, but the productive, life-giving force of its capacity for redistribution and renewal.

5. What if grace is immanent?

In network theology, an understanding of grace as an external, sovereign intervention is out of place. The model of a transcendent, sovereign power would be apt only if God were a king perched at the top of a cosmic hierarchy rather than a servant whose power resides in his solidarity with the poor and the outcast. What, then, might be an immanent notion of grace appropriate to a flat, network cosmology?

Here, grace can be understood as a systemic excess produced by the complexity of a network's ongoing, local interactions. In other words, grace is an emergent property of a self-organizing system. Or, again: it is the unintended remainder of an unbalanced equation. This kind of "free," emergent excess—an excess that cannot be wholly accounted for by any individual relations or locally intended consequences—is essential to the success of any truth. Truths overwrite banked knowledge by bringing into play the excess of a grace. By tracing novel pathways in light of a grace, truths open new network connections and new possibilities for productive interaction. It is this essentially productive aspect of any truth that ties truths to grace and grace to the promise of life (and renewed life) that is the heart of the Christian proclamation.

As a grace, Jesus's sacrifice is a precisely positioned catalyst that produces, in properly nonlinear fashion, an effect entirely out of proportion to itself because of its proximity to a network tipping point. Network thinking prompts us to set aside a "punitive" model of atonement appropriate to a sovereign, Platonic God and proposes instead a "display" theory of atonement. I have elsewhere explored how Paul's letter to the Romans elaborates a theory of justification that might be read in this way.[1] The core of this network theory of atonement is Paul's description in Romans 3:24–26 of how God's grace comes

> through the deliverance that is in Christ Jesus, whom God publicly displayed [*proetheto*] as a propitiation by his blood, through faith. He did this to display [*eis endeixin*] his righteousness, because in his divine forbearance he had passed over the sins previously committed; he did it to display [*endeixin*] in the present, pregnant moment his righteousness, and that he is upright and justifies the one who has faith in Jesus. (Rom. 3:24–26; my translation)

The King James translation of these verses tends to obscure what I think is plain in the Greek text. Paul repeatedly describes Jesus's sacrifice as a salvific "display" of what, in a sinful world, is otherwise purposefully obscured: God's righteousness (or unconditional solidarity) with the

---

1. See Adam Miller, *Badiou, Marion and St Paul: Immanent Grace* (London: Continuum, 2008), 21–64.

world. Jesus's atonement produces new life because it displays with full force the unaccountable strength of God's solidarity with the multitude.

6. What if the soul is a network?

My final question asks us to consider what it might mean if Christianity were to break with Platonism and describe the soul itself as a multitude. What if, rather than marking the limits of what is most uniquely and autonomously my own, the soul were an open, distributed system?

In this light, rather than being a sovereign, self-identical atom, the soul is a web of social relations, linked to itself only through the shared symbolic and affective pathways that loop my consciousness through the eyes of others. The soul, as a network, is given to itself only in and by its relationships, relationships that precede, both logically and temporally, its relation to itself. Looped, distributed, and radically dependent on (and, thus, *responsible for*) others, it is easy for a soul to be afraid. Sin is a soul's timid attempt to withdraw itself from the network that it is. Sin is the soul's comforting fantasy of a sovereign self. Souls are saved from sin by grace, by truths that overrun our imagined borders, outstrip our individual intentions, and display us to ourselves as the open networks that we are. Having faith is the work of affirming or consecrating—and then remaining faithful to—a truth's redistribution of our soul.

In the end, Paul's famous description of being divided against himself in Romans 7 may only make sense if the soul is a network. In this chapter, Paul despairs:

> I do not understand my own actions. For I do not do what I want, but I do the very thing I hate. Now if I do what I do not want, I agree that the law is good. But in fact it is no longer I that do it, but sin that dwells in me. For I know that nothing good dwells within me, that is, in my flesh. I can will what is right, but I cannot do it. For I do not do the good that I want, but the evil that I do not want is what I do. (Rom. 7:14–19, my translation)

Here, the soul, trying to act for its own sake and according to its own wishes, finds itself looped, distributed, and divided against itself. Salvation, however, is not produced through a "recovery" of the soul's fantasized autonomy but through a conscious abandonment of one's will to

Christ's. In a soul's faithful and affirmative abandonment of itself to network-being, Christ comes to live in us and we in him.

Further, if the soul is a localized network, then there is no such thing as individual salvation. Constituted as the soul that it is by its material, biological, symbolic, and affective connections to those nearest to it, salvation is a family affair. Salvation requires a productive distribution of our relationship with our parents and it is immeasurably enriched by a network bond between the sexes. If the soul is a network, then it becomes possible to offer theologically robust descriptions of human sexuality. And, moreover, if the soul is a network, then, as God covenants with Abraham (cf. Gen. 15:1–6), to be saved is to be endlessly faithful to our parents (and our parent's parents) and our children (and our children's children), because in the face of this complexity it is no longer possible to say where one soul ends and another begins.

Chapter 10

Jesus, Trauma, and Psychoanalytic Technique

By jointly reflecting on Bruce Fink's *Fundamentals of Psychoana-lytic Technique*[1] together with Marcus Pound's *Theology, Psychoanalysis, Trauma*,[2] my aim is to address in general what Lacanian psychoanalysis might teach us about religion. To set the stage, I offer a brief psychoanalytic reading of a passage from the Gospel of Mark.

1. Overture

Curiously, in the Gospel of Mark, Jesus is willfully secretive about being the messiah. He speaks in parables so that his audience "may see and not perceive . . . hear and not understand" (Mark 4:12). He miraculously heals a leper and then sternly warns him "to say nothing to anyone" (1:44). He orders unclean spirits to be silent about his identity (cf. 3:11–12). And even Jesus' own family, bewildered at his actions, think "he has gone out of his mind" (3:21).

Especially of note, though, are the events surrounding Peter's identification of Jesus as the messiah. On the road to Caesarea Philippi, Jesus questions his disciples: Who do people say that I am? They in turn respond with the local, speculative laundry list—John the Baptist, Elijah, or some other of the prophets—that says more about the speculators than it does about Jesus. Jesus then asks: "'But who do you say that I am?' Peter answered him, 'You are the Messiah.' And Jesus sternly ordered them not to tell anyone about him" (Mark 8:29–30).

---

1. Bruce Fink, *Fundamentals of Psychoanalytic Technique: A Lacanian Approach for Practitioners* (New York: W.W. Norton, 2007).

2. Marcus Pound, *Theology, Psychoanalysis, Trauma* (London: SCM Press, 2007).

Jesus' response to this bold confession is bluntly anti-climactic. He neither accepts nor rejects Peter's identification. Rather, he silences it. In short order, the reasons for Jesus' reticence become apparent: Peter's answer may be technically correct, but the logic that animates it remains damningly human (cf. Mark 8:33). Jesus is not the messiah Peter imagines him to be.

Avoiding Peter's nomination, Jesus instead responds by referring to himself as "the son of man" and begins to teach the disciples that he must "suffer many things, and be rejected by the elders and the chief priests and the scribes, and be killed, and after three days rise again" (Mark 8:31). This description is so deeply at odds with his image of the messiah that Peter immediately pulls Jesus aside and begins to rebuke him. Peter will have none of it: Jesus's oracle disavows rather than fulfills the messianic dream of triumph, glory, and satisfaction invested in him by Peter's identification.

Jesus, in turn, rebukes Peter. Peter may have uttered the truth about Jesus, but he has no right to presume any mastery of that confession's meaning. Systematically, Jesus upends messianic expectations: "If someone desires to follow after me, let them deny themselves, and take up their cross, and follow me" (Mark 8:34). Jesus, as the messiah, has not come to confirm us, fulfill our fantasies, or normalize our inadequacies. Instead, he comes to provoke desire, induce self-denial, and incite a reassessment of the crosses that we bear. In refusing us the balm that an easy identification with his divinity might provide, Jesus offers instead the difficulty of something real. Rather than mirroring Peter's self-congratulation, Jesus plainly prophesies what that mirror image is meant to hide: the imminence of suffering, rejection, and death.

However, in doing so, Jesus means to turn the tables on death. "Those who want to save their lives will lose them, and those who lose their lives for my sake and for the sake of the good news, will save them. What does it profit them to gain the whole world and forfeit their own lives?" (Mark 8:35–36). Jesus is not going to play the game. He's not going to abide by the rules of everyday discourse. He's not going to project or confirm any images of wholeness or sufficiency. Rather, his intention is to lose what is found and find what is lost. When identified, he'll sidestep the identification. When speaking, he'll speak in such a way as to provoke misunderstanding. When spoken to, he'll show the speaker what they didn't mean to say. Throughout, Jesus's aim is to shift the register of discourse away from "human things," from the shelter of images that invite only rivalry or identification, and toward the defenseless divinity of the real (Mark 8:33).

Eluding facile reciprocity, Jesus gives us to hear precisely what everyday discourse means to silence: alienation, suffering, and death. But, in salvific disequilibrium, he means for alienation, suffering, and death to be heard otherwise than we fear. He means for us to hear them as openness, grace, and life itself.

2. The Fundamentals of Technique

Lacanian psychoanalysis resonates with and separates out a certain kind of religious discourse. It induces this difference because its theoretical categories and clinical methodologies pose a definitive question about the relation of any religious discourse to the desires that animate it. Lacan's work forces the question: is a given religious discourse a reactionary defense against the real or does it tend toward an exposure of it? In brief, is a given discourse oriented by the imaginary or the symbolic?

Classically, the psychoanalytic line on religion has been numbly consistent. Religion is taken with little equivocation as an obvious example of how to avoid the real through an imaginative fabrication of unity and sufficiency. God, the religious equivalent of an infinitely applicable band-aid, comes to save the ego from an endless variety of fragmentations and impending dissolutions. However, as accurate as this assessment may generally be (and we ought to be very careful in cavalierly dismissing the importance of such palliatives and band-aids), it is not difficult to see—especially in light of the *efficacy* of the psychoanalytic critique—that something essentially religious remains unaccounted for and, more importantly, that this something persists precisely because it wanders free among the very concepts and practices that psychoanalysis has reserved for itself.

The contours of this shared religious/psychoanalytic space come into sharper focus when the clinical rather than theoretical dimensions of Lacan's work are emphasized. Here, Bruce Fink's substantial and accessible explications of Lacanian practice are invaluable. While Fink's *A Clinical Introduction to Lacanian Psychoanalysis*[3] is without peer in pro-

---

3. Bruce Fink, *A Clinical Introduction to Lacanian Psychoanalysis: Theory and Technique* (Cambridge: Harvard University Press, 1999).

viding the necessary background, his recently published *Fundamentals of Psychoanalytic Technique: A Lacanian Approach for Practitioners* is similarly useful. Though *Fundamentals of Psychoanalytic Technique* lacks the theoretical heft of either *A Clinical Introduction* or Fink's *The Lacanian Subject: Between Language and Jouissance*,[4] its more practical and popular aims have their own virtues. Fink explicitly casts the new book as intended for clinicians who may have little or no prior acquaintance with Lacan and devotes it to "elementary technique" rather than "long theoretical explanations."[5] Though the losses incurred by such foreshortening are predictable, the lightness of Fink's theoretical touch nonetheless produces the welcome effect of clearing a practical path directly into the heart of Lacan's work. In short, Fink's descriptions of the aims and techniques of actual Lacanian practice go a long way toward showing why one might care about Lacan (despite his famed inaccessibility) in the first place. In itself, this effect is no small accomplishment.

Fink organizes his treatment of the most common psychoanalytic techniques[6] around the difference between two ways of hearing: one way of hearing attends to the imaginary dimension of what is said, the other gives itself to the symbolic dimensions of those same statements. All discourse is intelligible in either of these registers. Where the imaginary mode settles meanings into predictable and univocal patterns, the symbolic mode of listening proliferates meanings, calls the imaginary into question, and opens onto the real. Though the give and take of everyday discourse occurs primarily in the imaginary register, the aim of the psychoanalyst is to confront the patient (or analysand) with the symbolic dimensions of what typically goes unheard in their own discourse.

To facilitate this, analysts must themselves learn to listen in a way that is not simply reflexive. They must learn to see something other than their own image in what the analysand says in order to point out or punctuate this same something "other" for the analysand. As Fink explains:

> Our usual way of listening is highly narcissistic and self-centered, for in it we relate everything other people tell us to ourselves. We compare ourselves to them, we assess whether we have had better or worse

---

4. Bruce Fink, *The Lacanian Subject: Between Language and Jouissance* (Princeton: Princeton University Press, 1996).

5. Fink, *Fundamentals of Psychoanalytic Technique*, ix.

6. It should be noted that my discussion of psychoanalytic techniques, like Fink's, deals almost exclusively with those that are appropriate to the treatment of neurosis.

experiences than they have, and we evaluate how their stories reflect upon us and their relationship with us, whether good or bad, loving or hateful. This, in a word, is what Lacan refers to as the *imaginary* dimension of experience. The analyst as listener is constantly comparing and contrasting the other with herself and constantly sizing up the other's discourse in terms of the kind of *image* it reflects back to her.[7]

Most discursive exchanges are dominated by this imaginary dimension. Everyday discourse largely consists of mutually oblique feedback loops structured dyadically by identification or rivalry in which participants primarily register only their own concerns. Further, Fink argues, this short-circuiting of intersubjectivity by the imaginary extends even (and, perhaps, *especially*) to moments of "empathy" and "understanding" where we identify the feelings or experiences of the other person with our own. Thus, he claims, therapies that are guided by this kind of imaginative "empathy" and "understanding" are, ironically, much more likely to be about the analyst's self-image than the analysand's symptoms because, "at the imaginary level, the analyst's own personality takes center stage."[8]

The aim of analysis, then, is not to reshape the analysand in the image of the analyst. Nor is it to break-through the recursive mirror play that characterizes our relationships in order to facilitate an "objective" perspective or an "authentic" connection with other people. In this context, "objectivity" and "authenticity" are nearly always imaginary lures. Rather, by attending to the symbolic dimensions of the analysand's discourse, the aim of the analyst is to draw attention to those formal features of language (puns, metaphors, conflations, mispronunciations, etc.) that mean more than the analysand apparently intended. By persistently foregrounding the ubiquity of the formal or symbolic excess of the analysand's discourse (i.e., the signifier's freedom to produce meaning far beyond the scope of any intended signification) the analyst aims to induce in the analysand a new relation to the images or fantasies that order their experience of the world.

The induction of this new relation is broadly therapeutic. As noted, the imaginary is problematic insofar as it attempts to fabricate, through exclusion, a misleading sense of closure, unity, and wholeness. On Fink's account, an analysand's choice to enter analysis is often prompted by a

---

7. Ibid., 4.
8. Ibid., 188.

negative experience of this imaginary "unity" as a stifling limitation or oppressive compulsion. As a result, "the analyst's concern is to empha-size the partiality of the image—in other words, the degree to which the image includes only a part of [the analysand]."[9]

Those thoughts, dispositions, and desires unaccounted for or ac-tively excluded by the ego's image (i.e., those thoughts, dispositions, and desires that are "repressed" by the ego's sense of who it is or what it ought to be) can be illuminated by the analytic work of drawing attention to the symbolic excesses of the analysand's own discourse. Progress is made in analysis when the excess of an analysand's verbal equivocation connects with and articulates the excess that is "repressed" or excluded by the imaginary.

It is the analyst's job to listen for and then draw attention to these unconscious verbal equivocations. Primarily, the analyst draws attention to the symbolic dimensions of an analysand's discourse with techniques of "punctuation": "The analyst's task is to provide a slightly different punctuation, a punctuation that brings out meanings in the 'text' of the analysand's speech that had not been visible before."[10] An analyst might punctuate an analysand's statements through a simple but well-timed "hmm," through the reiteration of key words or phrases with an alteration of emphasis that draws out the formal ambiguities of the construction, or, more emphatically, through the technique of "scansion" in which an analyst abruptly ends a session, "effectively placing a period, exclamation mark, or question mark not just at the end of a sentence or at the end of a paragraph, but rather at the end of a section or chapter of text."[11] Each of these methods of punctuation are "explicitly designed to shake-up, call into question, or deconstruct a neurotic analysand's self-conception."[12]

These interpretive punctuations hit the mark when they connect with an analysand's "symptoms." "Symptoms," Fink explains, "represent the return of the repressed"[13] and they arise wherever an analysand re-presses the threat of something foreign or disruptive. Here, symptoms should be understood as any repetitive way of dealing with the nagging persistence of what exceeds the ego's short grasp. Essentially, a symp-

---

9. Ibid., 81.
10. Ibid., 37.
11. Ibid., 49.
12. Ibid., 53.
13. Ibid., 15.

tom is an iterated stance adopted by the analysand to deal with the excess of what is "other," whether this "other" is a threatening object, another person, or some kind of internalized yet foreign desire. In this sense, an ego is nothing but a crystallized collection of symptoms, an image of coherence produced by a person's more or less coordinated set of symbolic strategies for dealing with both the external and internal excesses of their world.

The analytic process draws out what has been repressed by more starkly defining the contours of an analysand's symptoms. Rather than presenting and defending a self-image and thereby engaging analysands at the level of the imaginary, analysts attempt to situate themselves primarily in the symbolic register by presenting an image that is elusive and enigmatic. They attempt to present themselves "more as a blank screen or 'mirror' than most other people in [the analysand's] life do, which presumably allows him to project and repeat more aspects of relationships and situations from the past with [the analyst] than he is able to do with colleagues, friends, and lovers."[14] By providing an occasion for the analysand to repeat in condensed fashion crucial aspects of their relationships with family, friends, colleagues, etc., the analyst is able to identify the basic coordinates of these iterated stances (or symptoms) and systematically call into question their partiality.

As Fink indicates, Freud famously defined this analytic process of repetition as "transference." According to Freud, transference names that process where "a whole series of psychological experiences are revived, not as belonging to the past, but as applying to the person of the physician at the present moment."[15] In the course of analysis, the analysand will assign the analyst to any number of "preexisting positions" in their psychical economy, identifying the analyst as a friend, enemy, colleague, parental figure, potential lover, etc. The assignment of the analyst to these preexisting positions corresponds in the analysand to the variety of iterated stances or symptoms the analysand has adopted over time for the sake of dealing with the repressed excess of the other.[16] (Further, as is well known, Freud classically identified the most important of these repetitive stances with those that are originally and Oedipally shaped by our relationship to our parents.) Thus, in

---

14. Ibid., 135.
15. Quoted in Fink, *Fundamentals of Psychoanalytic Technique*, 126.
16. See ibid., 148.

transference, the analysand "transfers" a series of positive and/or negative reactions into their relationship with the analyst (depending on
the symbolic structure of the symptom) to which the analyst's assigned
position then correlates. Essentially, the analysand assigns the analyst a
role and in response to this assigned role the analysand then plays out
their own designated part.

It is in the interpretation of this transference that the unconscious,
symbolic dimensions of the analysand's discourse are put to work for
the sake of truth. In relation to analysis, the term "truth" has a very
precise meaning. Here, Fink argues, truth "is not so much a property of
statements as it is a relationship to the real."[17] Fundamentally, the "real"
is simply the unsymbolized. The real is both what the univocity of the
imaginary excludes and what the equivocation of the symbolic suggests.
As a relationship to this real, truth occurs when a new relationship is
produced for the analysand between what has been repressed and what
has gone unheard in their own speech.

> *Truth, as experienced by the analysand in the analytic context, has to do
> with what remains to be said, with what has not yet been said.* What has
> already been said often seems empty, whereas what is being said now
> for the first time is what has the potential to shake things up, is what
> feels important, truthful. To the analysand, *the truth is always elsewhere*:
> in front of him, yet to be found. Insofar as it concerns "what remains
> to be said," truth in psychoanalysis has to do with the experience of
> symbolizing what has never before been put into words. With Lacan,
> I refer to "what has never before been put into words" as "the real."[18]

A psychoanalytic interpretation is true when, noting the position of an
analysand's symptoms, it "hits" the unsaid real and makes a connection
between the previously unheard excess of what the analysand had already been saying and that repressed excess that the analysand's image
excludes. Analysis is "true" when the analysand sees the truth of what
they had unintentionally said. The production of this new connection
with the real has the potential, depending on the situation, to either
subtly or dramatically reorganize the symbolic coordinates that pattern
an analysand's relational dispositions. In other words, hitting the real
can reorganize an analysand's symptoms.

---

17. Ibid., 77.
18. Ibid., 76.

In the end, the work of producing this "truth" must be performed by the analysand and can only be facilitated by the analyst. The analyst, as Socratic midwife, simply aims to induce in the analysand the birth of a truth by prompting a connection, however partial, between the real and the symbolic. Indeed, the only power at the disposal of psychoanalysis is this power of speech to distract our preoccupation with the imaginary and connect the real with the symbolic. The "talking cure" must be a *talking* cure" because its efficacy rests in its ability to get the analysand to shift discursive registers and hear the unintended truths that their symptoms have been pronouncing. Fink continues:

> It is in the impact that speech is able to have on the real that lies the power of psychoanalysis. Left to its own devices, the real does not change over time; like a traumatic war experience, it persists, insistingly returning in nightmares or even waking life . . . . It is only by symbolizing it in words—and in many cases it must be articulated a number of times in different ways—that one can begin to shift positions with respect to it.[19]

The real, unassimilated by the diachronic narrative that unfolds in our daily interactions, desires, and fantasies, has a kind of eternal or synchronic power of persistence. Unspoken, it continues, out of time, to unconsciously shape our relationships and prompt the repetition of our symptoms as we avoid it.

Lacanian psychoanalysis hypothesizes that there is typically an underlying pattern that organizes in general our symptoms or fantasies and that this underlying pattern "defines the subject's most basic relation to the Other."[20] This underlying pattern is called a "fundamental fantasy." Fink's description of what constitutes a fundamental fantasy is particularly clear:

> Neurotics each have a fundamental fantasy that organizes their relation with others and with the world in general. While we each have many different conscious fantasies, the majority of them can be seen to follow a similar scenario in which we cast ourselves in a particular role, as a victim of other's punitive passions, as an object desired by or used by others, as a user of other people, or as a hero who saves victims, for example. Our individual fundamental fantasy colors the way we see the world and interact with it, leading us to create and recreate

19. Ibid., 77.
20. Ibid., 123.

the same kind of scenario, the same kind of relationship with others again and again.[21]

The work of analysis draws to a conclusion when a sufficient number of new connections have been made for the analysand to be fundamentally resituated in relation to the real. This shift in relation to the real allows new kinds of relationships and interactions to unfold between the analysand, the analysand's own desires, and other people.

It is important to remember, though, that this kind of analysis does not end when the patient is judged by the analyst to finally be whole, healthy, or normal. To judge the outcome of an analysis in these terms would amount to re-immersing the analysand in the imaginary. Rather, the transformation of an analysand's fundamental fantasy involves a basic acknowledgement of their *essential* incompletion. Traversing a fundamental fantasy involves a shift in the analysand's relation to the desires that de-complete them: rather than simply attempting to satisfy their desires once and for all through the fulfillment of specific demands, the analysand comes to take desire itself as something to be claimed and desired. Or, rather than simply fabricating an imaginary wholeness, the analysand comes to confess the imaginary for the image that it is. In this sense, the aim of analysis is not to eliminate all of an analysand's symptoms but to reorganize them in such a way as to include their partiality as a feature that the system itself takes into account.

3. Divine Trauma

Thus far, I have only obliquely indicated the connection between Lacanian psychoanalysis and certain kinds of religious discourse. Mark's exemplary description of Jesus as a willfully secret messiah and Bruce Fink's elaboration of psychoanalytic techniques have only been roughly juxtaposed. Fortunately, much of the work needed to explicitly thread them together has already been done by Marcus Pound's new book *Theology, Psychoanalysis, Trauma*.

Pound's work is much needed in light of the interest that Slavoj Žižek's engagement with Christian thinking has generated over the past few years, and his book offers a clear, concise, and well-documented argument that, in order to appreciate the significance of the space shared by religion and psychoanalysis, it is important to read Lacan

---

21. Ibid., 227.

in light of Kierkegaard. Pound's position is that Lacan's often facile critique of religion as a neurotic defense against the real obscures the substantial debt owed by psychoanalytic practices to Christian theology. A reconsideration of Kierkegaard's treatment of faith, anxiety and repetition draws out both the direct and indirect genealogical debts of Lacan's project. Pound argues that "where Lacan takes religion as a knee-jerk reaction to semiotic uncertainty and the ensuing anxiety, Kierkegaard takes Christianity as the only means by which one can be truly uncertain."[22] In short, "Kierkegaard's aims and methods are commensurate with Lacanian analysis inasmuch as both employ an indirect approach to the subject aimed at cultivating the subjective appropriation of truth."[23] As a result, in order to adequately address religion, psychoanalytic thought must take into account the way that many religious practices are self-consciously designed to break with the imaginary and generate the anxiety that accompanies contact with the real. Here, Pound holds, "Christ's traumatic intervention is the paradigm of the analytic intervention."[24]

Pound squares Lacan with Kierkegaard on two fronts: (1) he aligns Lacan's triumvirate of basic theoretical categories (the imaginary, the symbolic, and the real) with Kierkegaard's own conceptual trinity (the aesthetic, the ethical, and the religious), and (2) he reads clinical psychoanalysis as a secular version of the classically Christian practice of typological repetition.

The first set of alignments is straightforward and the fit is relatively convincing. Kierkegaard's aesthetic stage is dominated by the play of passions, the dyadic mirroring of rivalry or identification, and the expression of desire in terms of specific demands in need of satisfaction. The milieu of the aesthete is the imaginary. The ethical corresponds to Lacan's symbolic in that both involve the primacy of law and language, the triangulation of relationships, and the rule of "universal" judgments. Finally, as Pound puts it, "the religious stage corresponds directly to the real, because in the religious sphere one identifies with the exception that grounds the rule; i.e., that which is ceded as condition of entry into the symbolic; the constitutive exception of the law."[25]

22. Pound, *Theology, Psychoanalysis, Trauma*, 94.
23. Ibid., 154.
24. Ibid., 142.
25. Ibid., 104.

Here, however, it is Pound's reading of psychoanalytic practice as an attempt to induce a kind of typological repetition that is of particular interest. With an eye on Kierkegaard's notion of repetition, Pound describes Lacan's conception of the symptom in compatible terms. Symptoms, as we've already seen, are a repetition of past events or relationships. They circle back to and repeat in the present moment a previously adopted stance meant to stave off some traumatic excess. The structure of a symptom is such that, in its repetition, it often "sheds new light on a past event, illuminating meaning in different ways."[26] Or, even better, Pound describes the symptom's iteration as what "articulates the trauma through a difference."[27] Symptoms are the key to psychoanalytic treatment because they produce both similarity and difference: they repeat the same defensive stance again and again *but* they do so each time in a different context with different players. Through punctuation and interpretation, the analyst works to bring forward the excess of this difference already present in the analysand's iterated symptom and, thus, effect a connection with the real around which the symptom has been circling. Summarizing this point, Pound concludes:

> Just as a symptom is structured through repetition, so is the cure. Through analysis one challenges past meaning with a view to releasing one for action in the present. Indeed, the goal of analysis is for the analysand to repeat himself on the basis of a difference, that is, to act in a manner that is not circumscribed by his neurosis or a particular pattern of behavior.[28]

This freedom to act in a manner not circumscribed in advance by one's symptoms marks a shift in the structure of an analysand's fantasies and a transformation of their relation to the meaning of past events. In this way, analysis is fundamentally the work of "challenging the assumption that the past is irretrievably behind us."[29]

In a Christian context, repeating the past with a difference is called typology. According to Paul, for instance, Christ comes as a salvific antitype who repeats with a difference the structure and meaning of Adam's originally traumatic dependence on God (cf. Rom. 5:12–21). Taking this example as a pattern, typology comes to serve in general

---

26. Ibid., 63.
27. Ibid., 64.
28. Ibid.
29. Ibid., 143.

as "the basis for a Christian understanding of the relation between the Old Testament and the New Testament: the Old Testament is retroactively reconfigured by the presence of Christ."[30]

However, Pound's treatment of typology in the context of psychoanalytic therapy is especially productive because it clarifies the function of types: rather than being a hermeneutic parlor trick performed for the benefit of the faithful, types are fundamentally mechanisms for effecting salvific change. A retroactive reconfiguration of the past that frees an individual from the tyranny of their symptoms and shifts their relation to the real by repeating the past with a difference *is* an experience of grace and repentance.

Further, typology offers itself as a particularly appealing model of grace because it takes seriously the immanence and materiality of history. As Pound emphasizes, typological readings are *not* allegories: "Typology is distinct from allegory in that the historical significance of the narrative is not overlooked in favour of a spiritual or eternal truth."[31] In typology, both type and antitype are specific, concrete historical events. Salvation is not effected through the subsumption of a past event by a general and transcendent spiritual truth. Rather, our symptomatic relation to past events can be transformed only through the intervention of another concrete event. This new event may set in motion a systematic reordering of history, but such a reconfiguration works to produce a typological salvation *of* history rather than a kind of vaguely spiritual salvation *from* history.

In other words, as in analysis, a typological conception of grace does not save us from the uncertainty of our temporality or the anxiety of our perpetual incompletion; rather it relates us to this incompletion in a novel way that counts its own temporality as *essential* to life and freedom. A reordering of the symbolic coordinates that structure our relation to the real allows for a reevaluation of our lack of unity and completion. From this new position, "anxiety ceases to be a category of despair, taking instead the form of grace."[32]

Pound's book culminates with a psychoanalytic interpretation of the Eucharist. In the end, Pound says, "the wager of this work is that if the Church is to communicate the mystery of transubstantiation with-

---

30. Ibid., 64.
31. Ibid., 65.
32. Ibid., 75.

in our cultural milieu, then psychoanalysis, and in particular Jacques Lacan's postmodern variation, provides the most coherent language."[33] In the context of the Sacred Mass, God functions as an "arch-analyst" whose "love for man leads him to fashion an indirect yet incisive intervention into time through the work of Christ."[34] In what sense does the Eucharist figure a kind of psychoanalytic intervention? In the course of a Mass, the narcissism of the participants' imaginary identifications are called into question as a connection is forged between the symbol of the bread and the traumatic real of Christ's inassimilable body. Here, "Christ's repeated intervention in the Sacred Mass may be seen in terms of analytic intervention, and hence the Sacred Mass may be seen in terms of a social form of analysis."[35]

This last parallel, however, seems to function more by way of rough analogy than strict homology. The theoretical similarities between psychoanalytic techniques and a Christian understanding of typology are relatively tight and specific, but Pound's attempt to map—at a practical level—the experience of an individual analysis onto the shared experience of the Eucharist necessarily calls for a more creative fit.

As Fink's book makes clear, the efficacy of analysis is grounded almost entirely in the sustained specificity of an individual's interaction with an analyst whose entire aim is to position themselves in such a way as to incite a systematic reconfiguration of their symptoms. Something analogous might take place in a Mass, but it is questionable whether or not anything like "a social form of analysis" could be individually efficacious and it is even more suspect that the power of the experience would derive from a participant who is left more or less to the work of *self-analysis* in the absence of a concrete interlocutor capable of pressing them on the details of their symptoms and transferences.

Most importantly, the analogy seems to fail in this respect: the beating heart of psychoanalytic practice is its demand that the analysand *speak*. To what extent would a "talking cure" remain essentially psychoanalytic if it did not require the analysand to talk, and this in immense detail and at great length? In the context of the Eucharist, however, there is no such occasion for speech.[36] If one were to look

---

33. Ibid., xiii.
34. Ibid., 141.
35. Ibid., 142.
36. A final note: if, as I mentioned in an earlier footnote, most everything dis-

for something more specifically like a psychoanalytic practice in the context of Christian worship, it may be more readily identifiable in the difficult and detailed work of being confronted by what exceeds us in performatively reading (and even writing) sacred texts.

4. Conclusion

Nonetheless, Pound's work makes a convincing case for what I take to be the central issue: that there exists a theoretical—and, perhaps, practical—space that is shared by a certain kind of religious discourse and Lacanian psychoanalysis. The mapping of this space is productive in that it (1) situates the aims and practices of psychoanalysis within the broader context of our common traditions while (2) simultaneously illuminating the extent to which the psychoanalytic critique of religion does (and does not) hit the mark. However, it is in this latter respect that mapping their overlay may be of greatest practical use. The ability of psychoanalytic theory to separate out a certain kind of religious discourse whose aim is to expose us to the real may prove valuable in a broad assessment of religious practices.

---

cussed here in terms of Lacanian technique applies primarily to the treatment of neurotics, then what of everyone else? Granted, most people may fit the category of neurosis, but in what sense might religious practices (or, say, the Eucharist in particular) induce the intervention of grace for psychotics? This is not a problem peculiar to Pound's work but marks, instead, a problem of broad importance that will eventually need to be addressed by anyone attempting to think about religion practices in psychoanalytic terms.

Chapter 11

Every Truth is a Work,
Every Object is a Covenant

It seems to me that the truthfulness of the Book of Mormon is a work to be done, not a fact in evidence. The book is more like a field to be plowed than a fruit to be eaten. You're not supposed to keep it on your nightstand with the other books you're not reading, you're supposed to tear out its pages, plant them in your yard, and see what grows. Bound by covenant, it is our work to *make* the Book of Mormon be true in as many ways and in as many worlds as we are able.

Clearly, this way of talking breaks with some common sense assumptions about truth. It runs afoul of two assumptions in particular: (1) that there is *one* neatly preformatted world shared by all, and (2) that truths are then just accurate reflections of what has already been decided.

Forget this picture for a moment. Drawing on the work of Bruno Latour, let's experiment with a different model. Taking a metaphysical cue from Joseph Smith, let's begin instead by assuming a plurality of co-eternal agents. Further, let's claim (1) that agency goes all the way down such that "to exist" is "to be an agent," (2) that agents are not timeless, self-contained atoms but messy, dynamic assemblages of other agents, (3) that a world is an active assemblage of agents, not a preformatted container, and (4) that there are, as a result, worlds without number.

On this model, truths are not reflections of the one true world. Rather, truths are one way of talking about the hard work of making new worlds and assembling new coalitions of agents. Truth-making is the work of creation. It is ontological rather than epistemological. It is the work of building bridges between agents who do not come pre-assembled and of binding those agents together by way of covenants. Truths are promises faithfully kept, they are coalitions painstakingly maintained.

Let's try this with the Book of Mormon. Because it exists, the Book of Mormon is an agent. While available for engagement, the book has a trajectory of its own that resists assimilation, imposes costs, and bends the lines taken by other agents. The book has gravitational pull. The Book of Mormon is not a timeless, self-contained atom but a work in progress composed of overlapping sets of only partially compatible agents. The book is a moving target. It is a messy intersection of words, histories, poems, failures, talismans, plates, prophecies, agendas, blue-and-gold covers, translations, super-thin scripture-paper pages that tear when you turn them and bleed through when you mark them, prejudices, criticisms, international copyrights, ink, politics, lost manuscripts, angels, etc. The Book of Mormon is a world composed of worlds and it is available for the making of new worlds.

But on its own account, the Book of Mormon is, above all, a covenant. It is a covenant cast in the form of a record. Like all agents, the Book of Mormon is an abridgment of other agents. As the title page indicates, "it is an abridgment of the record of the people of Nephi, and also of the Lamanites." It is an "abridgment taken from the Book of Ether also, which is a record of the people of Jared, who were scattered." The book *is* a remnant written *for* "a remnant of the house of Israel." Its work is to catalyze a gathering of scattered agents, to show them "what great things the Lord hath done for their fathers" so that "they may know the covenants of the Lord, that they are not cast off forever." This book is a concrete manifestation of those promises made to the fathers that their children would not be lost, and it is a vehicle for the fulfillment of that promise. In particular, the book is an angel, a messenger, an agent working on behalf of other agents, bound by covenant to convince both "Jew and Gentile that JESUS is the CHRIST, the ETERNAL GOD, manifesting himself unto all nations."

The Book of Mormon is a basin of attraction. It curves the fabric of space-time and draws us into relation. It is a voice from the dust, arresting our attention. It makes claims on us and invites us to claim it in return. We are free to denounce it, discount it, or make truths out of it—but, to the extent that our paths intersect, we are not free from the hazard of its pull. Section 84 of the Doctrine and Covenants presses the book's claim.

> And by this you may know they are under the bondage of sin, because they come not unto me. For whoso cometh not unto me is under the

bondage of sin. And whoso receiveth not my voice is not acquaint-
ed with my voice, and is not of me. And by this you may know the
righteous from the wicked, and that the whole world groaneth under
sin and darkness even now. And your minds in times past have been
darkened because of unbelief, and because you have treated lightly the
things you have received—Which vanity and unbelief have brought
the whole church under condemnation. And this condemnation
resteth upon the children of Zion, even all. And they shall remain
under this condemnation until they repent and remember the new
covenant, even the Book of Mormon and the former commandments
which I have given them, not only to say, but to do according to that
which I have written—That they may bring forth fruit meet for their
Father's kingdom; otherwise there remaineth a scourge and judgment
to be poured out upon the children of Zion. (vv. 50–58)

As an agent, the Book of Mormon manifests as a voice that claims us.
To refuse this claim, to treat this claim lightly, is to be bound by sin.
Bound by sin, our bodies groan and our minds grow dark. Our vanity has brought the whole church under condemnation. The Book of
Mormon is not only something to say, it is something to be done. The
book is a promise to be kept, a claim to be magnified, a covenant to be
honored. Remember the new covenant, even the Book of Mormon.
The promises made to *its* fathers must be planted in the hearts of *our*
children to bring forth fruit meet for the Father's kingdom. Otherwise
the children will be scattered.

In this respect, the Book of Mormon exemplifies what it means,
in general, to be a truth. Every object is an agent, every agent is a coalition, ever coalition is a truth, and every truth is a covenant. Truths, as
covenants, must be *made*. They must be built just as surely and just as ma-
terially as any freeway overpass or plumbed toilet. Truths are built by the
concretion of agents in a common cause. Truths are not slick, top-down,
univocal declarations but hard-won, bottom-up, multilateral settlements.

Some truths are big, some are small. Some truths are dependable,
some are fragile. Some truths are strong, some are weak. Some truths
are easily portable, some are genre-dependent. The measure of a truth
is not the passive vanity of an accurate reflection but the size, diversity,
and cohesion of the crowd of agents that can be gathered to compose
that truth and dependably endorse it. Let me repeat these criteria: the
strength of a truth is gauged by (1) the *quantity* of the agents gathered into its coalition, (2) the *diversity* of the agents (human and non-

human, living and nonliving, material and formal, cultural and natural) gathered into its coalition, and (3) the *durability* of the settlement that collects them. Truth is never all or nothing. There is no original "all" against which a truth can be measured and, so, truth is gauged instead by indexing its strength according to the quantity, diversity, and durability of its amassed support.

All truths are judged according to these same criteria. Science has no inherent advantage over poetry, history has no inherent advantage over mathematics, religion has no inherent advantage over politics, etc. All disciplines, despite variations in their strategies for coalition-building, must fashion the same kind of claim. They compete to fashion compromises capable of claiming as cooperators as many different kinds of agents as possible. Any truth that will fly is a truth that is, to whatever height it manages, true.

The world does not come preformatted. The world is a welter of competing agents and truth is a marketplace. When a truth emerges, it does so by negotiating cross-platform compatibilities from generally divergent arrays of actors. Truths invite assent, they gather signatures, and they abridge collections of agents into functional simplifications. Truths are never even entirely compatible with themselves let along with other truths. Every truth leaves a vast remainder. In this sense, a truth, as a covenant, is an operationalized simplification. It takes what is many and sets it to work as one.

Say you want to make the case that the arctic ice cap is not melting at an alarming rate. There is nothing to stop you from trying. But this claim will only be as true as the quantity and diversity of cooperators it can durably claim. Producing statements that only some *humans* find persuasive won't get you very far. If you want to speak truthfully about icebergs, then it is not enough to convince your fellow scientists, some influential politicians, or even a bevy of soccer moms. To have real traction you'll need enough research grants, measurements, instruments, photos, outposts, statistics, charts, satellites, etc. to convince the icebergs themselves to line up behind what you have to say. Similarly, if you want to make claims about honey, you're alignment of agents will have to queue not just bee-keepers, but flowers and hives and bees as well. The more bees that agree, the more substantial your claim becomes. Non-human actors get every bit as much a say in the composition of a truth as humans do. In fact, the durability of a truth depends primarily on the quantity of the *nonhuman* agents that counter-claim our work because nonhumans tend to be significantly less gullible than people are. People tend to be suckers—especially for authority. But when it comes to truth, appeals to authority carry only as much weight as the masses that such authority can muster. The work of making truths—the work engaged in by scientists, lawyers, teachers, doctors, politicians, religious leaders, and entrepreneurs alike—is simply to get out the vote. There are no metaphysical shortcuts for skirting this work.[1]

Say you want to make a normative claim about how things *should* be rather than a descriptive claim about how things *are*. The work is the same. Morals and values and obligations are truths that cannot be set aside. But, like all truths, they too are messy, historically situated, localized, ad hoc, and emergent covenants. They too are the provisional product of ongoing, bottom-up negotiations between however many agents are involved.

Say you want to offer a brilliant reading of Genesis that requires the Earth to be just six thousand years old. I have no objection to this. You are welcome to try. But it is not enough to convince a subset of humans to go along with your reading. Nonhumans must be convinced too. The opinion of a fossil matters. Carbon-14 gets a say. DNA has a voice. Geological formations can't be discounted. If 4.5 billion years worth of rocks and weather and radioactive decay disagree, then your reading is seriously hamstrung.[2]

The irony of a "literal" reading that discounts the material agency of actual rocks *and* actual words is that it flirts with nihilism. A reading of Genesis doesn't fail to be true if it fails to flawlessly repeat. It fails to be true when it no longer bothers to take both words and rocks seriously as *agents* with independent histories, trajectories, weaknesses, and frictions of their own. Reading is not qualitatively different from photosynthesis or mitosis or cloud formation. The measure of a biblical interpretation is simply: what agents does it convoke, how many, of what variety, and for how long? There is no original meaning to recover. There are only agents to be persuaded—again and again.

---

1. Compare, here, the whole of my chapter on "Truth" in *Speculative Grace: Bruno Latour and Object-Oriented Theology* (New York: Fordham University Press, 2013), 103–7.

2. Cf. ibid., 110–12.

The necessity of this work is not to be regretted. The world is not such that constructing truths takes us *farther* from the things themselves. And the world is not such that *extracting* ourselves from the messy work of making truths moves us closer to the things. Rather, because the real is itself characterized by a plurality of competing construction projects, a plurality of competing truths is just part and parcel of that ontological work that builds real bridges between real agents. Take science as an example. A multiplicity of competing and not entirely compatible scientific truths

> does not mean that scientists don't know what they are doing and that everything is just fiction, but rather [it means that we have to be able] to pry apart exactly what the ready-made notion of "natural objective matters of fact" had conflated too fast, namely reality, unity, and indisputability. When you look for the first, you don't automatically get the two others. And this has nothing to do with 'interpretive flexibility' allowed by 'multiple points of view' taken on the 'same' thing. *It is the thing itself that has been allowed to be deployed as multiple* and thus allowed to be grasped through different viewpoints.[3]

The fact that our truths never do better than an only partially compatible multiplicity does not mean that we've failed to grasp the real because we failed to capture the simple "unity" of the world itself. Exactly the opposite is the case: if we do not begin with the metaphysical assumption that the world *is* a simple unity, then our multiplicity of only partially compatible truths becomes a token of the fact that we *are* connecting with the multiplicity of the real itself. The relativity and partial compatibility of our truths does not derive from our cracked *perception* of the real, it derives from the nature of the real itself. Truth is not an epistemological problem, it is an ontological work.

Back, then, to the Book of Mormon. The truthfulness of the Book of Mormon is itself a work to be done, not a fact in evidence. The Book of Mormon is an occasion for world-building, alliance-making, and covenant-keeping. Bound by covenant, it is our work to *make* the Book of Mormon be true in as many ways and in as many worlds as we are able. How many friends can the Book of Mormon make? How many agents can it queue? In what variety?

---

3. Bruno Latour, *Reassembling the Social: An Introduction to Actor-Network Theory* (New York: Oxford University Press, 2005), 116.

Don't assume that the Book of Mormon is or isn't historically true. History is not one thing. *Make* the Book of Mormon historically true in as many times and as many places and to whatever degree you're able. Shop it around the world. Do the research, visit the sites, search the texts, gather the agents. Sit the gathered agents down and hammer out as binding a multilateral settlement as the motley crowd will, in each instance, allow. There will never be perfect agreement. That's fine. Work harder. Gather more signatures. Promise more in return. Bind the Book of Mormon to nineteenth-century Americana, test its compatibility with axial-age Mesoamerican geography, deploy its claims in twenty-first-century South Africa, port its prophecies into first century Palestine. The book will *not* be a perfect fit. Whatever. There is no such thing. What *can* you build and how sturdy *can* you make it? How does adding the Book of Mormon to a given historical assemblage change the assemblage? Moreover, how does it change the Book of Mormon?

Don't assume that the Book of Mormon is or isn't scientifically plausible. *Make* the Book of Mormon scientifically plausible. Does its account of creation square with evolution? With Native American DNA? With geology on a scale of billions of years? With light years of empty space? Let them pollinate each other and see what new things grow.

What other kinds of truths can you make with the Book of Mormon? Can you make a ward with it? Songs? Chapels? Psychiatric treatments? Movies? Paintings? Pharmaceutical advances? Poetry? Political campaigns? Can you make a life with it? Can you step out of the zombie-like haze of anxiety and distraction you tend to live in by way of it? Can you make joy with it? Can you assemble the body of Christ? Circulate Spirit? Can you, as the Book of Mormon itself demands, make a family with it? Can you turn the hearts of the fathers to the children and the children to the fathers? Can you use it to keep the children from being cast off forever? Can you adapt and extend and strengthen the promises made to the fathers? Will you allow the book to claim you and counter-claim it in return?

The question isn't: is the Book of Mormon accurate? Does it harmonize with some simple, pristine, ready-made, pre-established real? The question is: given the claim and counter-claim of the covenant that mutually composes us, what kind of worlds can the book and I make and how many can those worlds gather in?

Chapter 12

The Body of Christ

Is the church true? This is an old question, a question that had a meaningful home in the context of nineteenth century American sectarianism. But for us, it seems, the question may be poorly posed. It doesn't capture, I think, what is at stake for my children in their exposure to Mormonism and, more, it seems ill-suited to the kind of existential burn that might compel us, even today, to ask it. It seems like a bad fit for the kind of answer we're generally after in a white-knuckled prayer.

It's not that the question is "wrong" or that it couldn't be answered affirmatively. The problem is that it's too *thin*. In a twenty-first century context—in a world driven by big data, neo-liberalism, and global capitalism—it's not a load-bearing question. It's too narrow a thing to support, all by itself, the weight of the lives we put at stake in asking it.

"Is the church true?" Framed like this, the basic religious question is an institutional question. It's the kind of question that an institution would teach its members to ask about that institution. It's an institutional question fit for answering certain kinds of (inevitable) institutional needs. Like correlation in general, it filters the gospel through an institutional lens with an eye to highlighting what seems best for maintaining and reproducing that institution.

More, it feels like the kind of question that's meant to set an enormous apparatus of inferences in motion—a deductive pyramid scheme where if X is true, then A, B, C, D, and E must also be affirmed—that will, with one fell swoop, reduce the scope of life to the span of just that one question and, thus, answer everything all at once and for all time. In this respect, it doesn't have the feel of a question that's meant to be used *as* a question. It feels, instead, like the kind of question you're usually meant to ask when you already know the answer. It feels inherently rhetorical. It feels like the kind of question a missionary is supposed to ask Mr. Brown, a Boolean question meant to force a binary response.

But one basic problem with these vast institutional machines of deduction, inference, and QEDs is that they tend to be fragile. If just one cog comes loose, the whole thing groans and grinds to a halt. The wagered "all" of its "all or nothing" risks, without further consideration, simply returning as its conclusion: "nothing."

It's in this sense especially that the question seems to me to be too thin to still dependably accomplish significant religious work. As it's formulated, the question has just two foci: an institution and truth. That is, it's a religious question that, when prioritized, implicitly assumes (1) that *the* religious question is fundamentally institutional in character (which church?), and (2) that *the* religious question is also fundamentally epistemological and veridical (which is correct?). When prioritized, it implicitly assumes that the decisive question in a religious life takes just this form: the verification of institutional bona fides.

Now, I'm not suggesting that verification isn't important and I'm certainly not arguing that the institutional church shouldn't be sustained. The church is true. I value it immensely and we'd be lost without it. But I am arguing that making our religious lives turn on our evaluation of "the truthfulness of the church" is not the best way to approach a religious life *or* to sustain the institution. It's asking the institution to bear a spiritual weight that it cannot—and was not designed to—bear. Only Christ can bear the weight of any question that deserves to occupy the center of a religious life. If we want to get the right kind of answer to our questions about the church, we shouldn't ask first about the church. We should ask about Christ.

If your life itself depends on the question you're asking, then ask a question that is rich enough to cover the whole span of that (messy, unfinished, broken, vulnerable) life. Rather than asking if the church is true, ask something like: Is this the body of Christ? Is Christ manifest here? Does his blood flow in these veins? Does his spirit breathe in these lungs? Does forgiveness flourish here? Is faith strengthened? Is hope enlivened? Is charity practiced? Can I see, here, the body of Christ?

This is an appropriately thick question, a load-bearing question. This is a question properly fitted, by Christ himself, to address the existential burn that could compel our asking. This is a question that is big enough to not only address issues of veridicality, but of the whole head and the whole heart. And not just these, but the arms, the legs, the feet, the fingers, the toes, the spleen, the bowels, and the loins. The body of Christ includes them all. It includes the beautiful and the ugly, the public and the private, the desirable and the foul, the wealthy and the destitute, the lost and the found.

Inquire into the body of Christ. And then, perhaps, be willing to say: Though I may not even know what it *means* to say that the Church is true, I'd stake my life on the fact that this is Christ's body, broken and shared, and that we are its members.

Chapter 13

Silence, Witness, and Absolute Rock: Reading Cormac McCarthy

His feet left cold wet traces on the polished stones that sucked up
and vanished like the tale of the world itself.

Where do we go when we die? he said.
I don't know, the man said. Where are we now?

—Cormac McCarthy

It's a truism to say that Cormac McCarthy's novels—novels like
Blood Meridian or *The Crossing* or *The Road*—court nihilism. I think this
is right but, in itself, it tells us nothing. The question is: granted that his
work skirts round that silent abyss, how does McCarthy, nonetheless,
go about writing it? And what does it mean if this nihilism can, despite
itself, be written?

For McCarthy, meaning isn't bone-deep. It's penumbral. Meaning
is a thin shadow cast by the mass of a meaningless world. It's a side effect of things seen that, in themselves, would otherwise be mute. Meaning isn't primary but derivative. It's a byproduct of the world's turning.
The world is not in the business of making meaning. Rather, the world
makes meaning the way donut shops make donut holes: as leftovers.

The trouble with these leftovers is that, though they manage
meaning, they invite a nihilism all their own. Meaning can itself be a
tool too-ready-to-hand. The problem, in this second scenario, is not the
absurdity of the world. Nor is the problem that meaning-maps inevitably get made. The problem is our tendency to believe that the world
must be baptized in maps in order to be saved. We tie ourselves up
in knots when we think that the business of making meaning *is* the

work of redemption when, in fact, it is probably generally closer to the opposite. Redemption hinges, often enough, on meaning's unmaking.

McCarthy's novels circle round just this problem. They orbit, ad infinitum, the silence ringing in the heart of things. This heart-silence pushes us to practice indirection. Meaning, like happiness, can't be directly pursued. You have to care for the world without demanding that it make you happy. And you have to attend to the world without demanding that it be meaningful. If you practice care and attention, then happiness and meaning may accrue as a byproduct. But if you act for the sake of happiness, it will vanish into thin air. And if you demand that life be meaningful, then that scrim of meaning evaporates.

Meaning and happiness both happen on the periphery. They happen in the corner of your eye and if you try to look straight at them, they dry up like a mirage. But if you can forget what you want and keep your eyes on the world as it passes away (and the world's inevitable reduction to ashes may be McCarthy's most insistent theme), then meaning may follow you and joy may temper you. If you try to save meaning by making it eternal, primary, or fundamental, you'll lose it. But if you're willing to lose it, you can save it. In this sense, the world asks a difficult thing. It asks that we be faithful *both* to the fact that the world is not its shadow of meaning *and* to the fact that it nonetheless casts one. We have to avoid both the nihilism of reducing the world to its shadow and the nihilism of denying that such meaning exists.

In what follows, I want to examine three types or figures in McCarthy's fiction, focusing especially on his Border Trilogy and *Blood Meridian*. These three figures are: (1) the dreamer who wants to reduce the world to its shadow by *replacing* things with words and maps, (2) the mute who wants to *deny* that the world casts any shadow of meaning, and (3) the witness who, *echoing* the world's heart-silence, allows meaning and joy to peripherally accrue.

1. The Dreamer

The first figure is the dreamer. Dreamers are nihilists who, in their zeal to make everything meaningful—to make meaning primary and fundamental rather than derivative and oblique—deny the world for the sake of the word. They deny the rock for the sake of its shadow. But without the absurdity of that absolute rock, no shadow gets cast.

The dreamer manifests a will to reduction that works by reducing the absurdity of the world to the familiarity of words.

Early in the first volume of The Border Trilogy, *All the Pretty Horses*, the novel's young protagonist, John Grady Cole, is set to leave town. His grandfather has died and the family's ranch is to be sold. If he wants to pursue the cowboy's vanishing way of life, he'll have to cross the border into Mexico and search for it there. Before leaving, he crosses paths with an old girlfriend. She tries to cajole him into agreeing that they can still be friends, but Cole won't have it. "He shook his head. It's just talk, Mary Catherine. I got to get on.' Challenging him, Mary Catherine responds, 'What if it is just talk? Everything's talk isn't it?' To which Cole simply replies, 'Not everything.'"[1] Mary Catherine's idea that "everything's talk" is an innocent version of the dreamer's nihilism that, while recognizing that words may be worth more than Cole allows, nonetheless profoundly undervalues the world's own mute mass.

Later in the novel, when Cole finds himself locked deep in a Mexican prison, he is himself, ironically, accused of the same naïve nihilism.

> Perez nodded thoughtfully. Even in a place like this where we are concerned with fundamental things the mind of the anglo is closed in this rare way. At one time I thought it was only his life of privilege. But it is not. It is his mind.
>
> He sat back easily. He tapped his temple. It is not that he is stupid. It is that his picture of the world is incomplete. In this rare way. He looks only where he wishes to see.[2]

Perez goes on to describes this kind of willful blindness as "superstition." Americans only see what they want to see. They dream of a world where rocks are not absolute. Their vision is highly selective. Their picture of the world is woefully incomplete. They flood the field of their vision with talk to compensate for what's missing. And this is the substance of their superstition. Superstition is the substitution of words for worlds. Americans, he says, want good and bad to be written into the heart of things. But good and bad are a shadow and not the thing. To think otherwise is ignorance.

> Americans have ideas that are not so practical. They think that there are good things and bad things. They are very superstitious, you know.

---

1. Cormac McCarthy, *All the Pretty Horses* (New York: Vintage Books, 1993), 28.
2. Ibid., 192.

You don't think there's good and bad things?

Things no. I think it is superstitious. It is the superstition of a god-less people.

You think Americans are godless?

Oh yes. Don't you?[3]

The dreamer's nihilism shows itself as superstition, as an investment of words and ideas with a power that is foreign to their character. Dreamers may draw all the maps and pictures of the world they like, adding all the labels and legends that please them, but these maps aren't the world.

The Trilogy circles back around to this same point in the third volume, *Cities of the Plain*. Here, Cole again gets tagged as a dreamer unwilling to look the world square in the face. "Your friend," a pimp tells Billy Parham, "is in the grip of an irrational passion."

Nothing you say to him will matter. He has in his head a certain story. Of how things will be. In this story he will be happy. What is wrong with this story?

You tell me.

What is wrong with this story is that it is not a true story. Men have in their minds a picture of how the world will be. How they will be in that world. The world may be many different ways for them but there is one world that will never be and that is the world they dream of.[4]

Unable to superstitiously transubstantiate shadows into things, we suffer a confusion of map and world. Thus confused, our maps may damn us as easily as save us. "It is rather that the picture of the world is all the world men know and this picture of the world is perilous. That which was given him to help him make his way in the world has power also to blind him to the way where his true path lies. The key to heaven has power to open the gates of hell."[5]

Where Cole risks this kind nihilism as a side-effect of his pursuit of love, judge Holden from McCarthy's *Blood Meridian* pursues this first brand of nihilism with full knowledge and for its own sake. Bald as a stone, seven feet tall, pale as a ghost, and a brilliant polymath, the judge is a bloody, sociopathic incarnation of the dreamer's will to reduce the world to words. His explicit aim is to map every rock onto

3. Ibid., 194–95.

4. Cormac McCarthy, *Cities of the Plain* (New York: Vintage Books, 1998), 134.

5. Ibid., 293.

its shadow and then reduce the rock itself to dust. He wants to know everything because, for him, knowledge is annihilation.

> Whatever exists, he said. Whatever in creation exists without my knowledge exists without my consent.
> He looked about the dark forest in which they were bivouacked. He nodded toward the specimens he'd collected. These anonymous creatures, he said, may seem little or nothing in the world. Yet the smallest crumb can devour us. Any smallest thing beneath yon rock out of men's knowing. Only nature can enslave man and only when the existence of each last entity is routed out and made to stand naked before him will he be properly suzerain of the earth.[6]

"The freedom of birds is an insult to me," he continues. "I'd have them all in zoos." "That would be a hell of a zoo," a man replies. "The judge smiled. Yes, he said. Even so."[7]

Wherever he goes, the judge carries with him a giant ledger, bound in leather. When his company of men is not indiscriminately scalping and butchering whole villages of Apaches and Mexicans, the judge likes to sketch indigenous flowers and butterflies. And when he's done, he pinches them between his fingers or grinds them into the dirt. On one occasion, the company camps in some Anasazi ruins. The judge is fascinated with the rock paintings.

> The rocks about in every sheltered place were covered with ancient paintings and the judge was soon among them copying out those certain ones into his book to take away with him. They were of men and animals and of the chase and there were curious birds and arcane maps and there were constructions of such singular vision as to justify every fear of man and the things that are in him. . . . When he had done and while there yet was light he returned to a certain stone ledge and sat a while and studied again the work there. Then he rose and with a piece of broken chert he scrappled away one of the designs, leaving no trace of it only a raw place on the stone where it had been. Then he put up his book and returned to camp.[8]

---

6. Cormac McCarthy, *Blood Meridian or The Evening Redness in the West* (New York: Modern Library, 1985), 207.

7. Ibid., 207–8.

8. Ibid., 180.

On another occasion, the judge carefully catalogues a whole array of artifacts that he's collected.

> In his lap he held the ledgerbook and he took up each piece, flint or potsherd or tool of bone, and deftly sketched it into the book. He sketched with a practiced ease. . . . When he had done he took up [an artifact] and turned in it in his hand and studied it again and then he crushed it into a ball of foil and pitched it into the fire. He gathered up the other artifacts and cast them also into the fire and he shook out the wagonsheet and folded it away among his possibles together with the notebook. Then he sat with his hands cupped in his lap and he seemed much satisfied with the world, as if his counsel had been sought at its creation.[9]

This is the dreamer's fantasy: that he *had* been consulted at the world's creation; that, by way of superstition, he can bind the world to the meanings he fashions for it as if the world had been, from the very start, meant for just such a binding. And, in the process of reducing the world to words and ash, words themselves, things in their own right, become a torture. They become a "phantom corpus," a "bodiless structure" that is "composed of nothing but the spoken word" and that leaves "no trace or residue or shadow in the living world."[10]

2. The Mute

The second figure of nihilism is the mute. Unlike the dreamer, the mute has lost hold of words and, rather than being reduced to meaning, the naked world threatens to impose itself as meaningless.

Stylistically, this figure draws our attention to one of the most striking features of McCarthy's prose. Though his novels—especially the Border Trilogy—are punctuated at certain intervals by long, complex stretches of reported dialogue, the remainder of the text is characterized by a bone-deep silence that can stretch for twenty pages at a time, pages that contain no dialogue and, more importantly, pages that offer no report of any character's thoughts, emotions, motivations, or internal mental monologue. Instead, McCarthy unspools uninterrupted descriptions of the bare material world and the mute movement of people through it, mixed with instances of his trademark, quasi-bibli-

---

9. Ibid., 146.
10. *Cities of the Plain*, 212.

cal, metaphysically-inflected brand of commentary-from-nowhere. The stunning effect is that you can spend an hour reading some of the best prose wrought in the past hundred years and come away with the distinct impression of having sat all that time in the profoundest silence.

The mute is characterized by this silence. Wordless, the mute is like "a dreamer who wakes from a dream of grief to greater sorrow yet."[11] The mute wakes from a nihilism of words to the nihilism of a world without them. For the mute, "the pin has been pulled from the axis of the universe. Whatever one takes one's eye from threatens to flee away. Such a man is lost to us. He moves and speaks. But he is himself less than the merest shadow among all that he beholds. There is no picture of him possible. The smallest mark upon the page exaggerates his presence."[12] Maps and pictures have become impossible. The mute, himself, has become less than the merest shadow because, absent meaning, he longer casts one, and without an axis of penumbral contrast, the world reels.

Where the dreamer seeks the mystery and superstition of meaning, the mute is abandoned to the ordinary. As the pimp in *Cities of the Plain* explains to Cole during the novel's climatic knife-fight:

> In his dying perhaps the suitor will see that it was his hunger for mysteries that has undone him. Whores. Superstition. Finally death. For that is what brought you here. That is what you were seeking. . . . That is what brought you here and what will always bring you here. Your kind cannot bear that the world be ordinary. That it contain nothing save what stands before one. But the Mexican world is a world of adornment only and underneath is very plain indeed. While your world—he passed the blade back and forth like a shuttle through a loom—your world totters upon an unspoken labyrinth of questions. And we will devour you, my friend. You and all your pale empire.[13]

The dreamer's pale empire of words and pictures is going to be devoured by the plainness of a world that, because it has no hidden meaning, has nothing to hide. It is a shadowless world of absolute surface. The dreamer cannot bear that the world be ordinary, but it is this same plainness that can absorb the dreamer's words without any echo.

The mute is a like a dead man who, despite the death of meaning, has continued to wander the earth. As Billy Parham struggles to make

---

11. Cormac McCarthy, *The Crossing* (New York: Vintage Books, 1995), 146.
12. Ibid.
13. *Cities of the Plain*, 253.

it back to America with his brother's dry bones, a gypsy tells him, "what men do not understand is that what the dead have quit is itself no world but is also only the picture of the world in men's hearts."[14] But, "the world cannot be quit for it is eternal in whatever form as are all things within it. In those faces that shall now be forever nameless among their outworn chattels there is writ a message that can never be spoken because time would always slay the messenger before he could ever arrive."[15]

The mute, like the dead, have not quit the world but only their picture of it. The world revolves nameless. Like *Blood Meridian's* company of bloody marauders, they wander through this world's desert waste, unnaming and nameless in it. "Above all else they appeared wholly at venture, primal, provisional, devoid of order. Like beings provoked out of the absolute rock and set nameless and at no remove from their own loomings to wander ravenous and doomed and mute as gorgons shambling the brutal wastes of Gondwanaland in a time before nomenclature was and each was all."[16]

3. The Witness

The third figure, more elusive than the others, is the figure of the witness. The witness safeguards both world and word through indirection. The witness has moved beyond the incantations of superstition and into the silence of worship. They are faithful *both* to the fact that the world is not its shadow, *and* to the fact that it nonetheless casts one. The witness gives silent witness to the heart-silence of the world.

In *Cities of the Plain*, John Grady Cole is told about what, as a witness, he should be listening for. The key is to take your cue from your horse.

> You'll see things in the desert at night that you cant understand. Your horse will see things. He'll see things that will spook him of course but then he'll see things that dont spook him but still you know he seen something.
> What sort of things?
> I dont know.
> You mean like ghosts or somethin?
> No. I dont know what. You just know he sees em. They're out there.

---

14. *The Crossing*, 413.
15. Ibid.
16. *Blood Meridian*, 180.

Not just some class of varmint?

No.

Not somethin that will booger him?

No. It's more like somethin he knows about.

But you don't.

But you don't. Yes.

The old man smoked. He watched the moon. No further birds flew. After a while he said: I aint talkin about spooks. It's more like just the way things are. If you only knew it.[17]

The witness must listen for the thing that the horse knows but he doesn't. The key is what the witness hasn't seen or pictured. This thing isn't supernatural. It's not the object of superstition. It's not a ghost or a spook or a varmint. It's not like that. "It's more like just the way things are. If you only knew it."

In *Blood Meridian*, Tobin, an ex-priest, argues for this same point in a conversation with the novel's sometime protagonist, know simply as "the kid." Tobin argues that the witness isn't empowered by some special learning or intellectual prowess.

It may be the Lord's way of showin how little store he sets by the learned. Whatever could it mean to one who knows all? He's an uncommon love for the common man and godly wisdom resides in the least of things so that it may well be that the voice of the Almighty speaks most profoundly in such beings as lives in silence themselves.

He watched the kid.

For let it go how it will, he said. God speaks in the least of creatures.

The kid thought him to mean birds or things that crawl but the expriest, watching, his head slightly cocked, said: No man is give leave of that voice. The kid spat into the fire and bent to his work.

I aint heard no voice, he said.

When it stops, Tobin said, you'll know you've heard it all your life. Is that right?

Aye.

The kid turned the leather in his lap. The expriest watched him.

At night, said Tobin, when the horses are grazing and the company is asleep, who hears them grazing?

Dont nobody hear them if they're asleep.

---

17. *Cities of the Plain*, 124.

> Aye. And if they cease their grazing who is it that wakes?
> Every man.
> Aye, said the expriest. Every man.[18]

The work of the witness depends on their ability to hear that sound, that rushing wind, that has been blowing through the world their entire lives. This sound is the sound of the world's own heart-silence, the silence of its absurdity and meaninglessness, of its absolute rock that, perhaps despite itself, nonetheless generates a murmur of meaning. "The ox," an old man tells Billy Parham, "was an animal close to God as all the world knew and that perhaps the silence and the rumination of the ox was something like the shadow of a greater silence, a deeper thought."[19] The silence of the witness is, like that of the ox, a shadow of a greater silence, a deeper rock.

But waking to this silence, witnessing it, isn't easy to do. Something must happen. Something unexpected that stops us and forces to see that our horse sees something that we don't. "Some halt-stitch," McCarthy says, "in the working of things" that leads us to consider "those heavens in whose forms men see commensurate destinies cognate to their own" and to recognize that those heavens "now seemed to pulse with a reckless energy. As if in their turning things had come uncottered, uncalendered," such that "there might even be some timefault in the record."[20] This is the door to that greater silence: a halt-stitch in our lives, a timefault in the heavens, a faltering of order and meaning that shows an abyss at the root of things.

There is, McCarthy tells us, a particular gesture that opens this door. The gesture cannot be performed, only witnessed. The person performing the gesture may well not even know what they've accomplished in you by way of it. *The Crossing*'s own ex-priest, holed up in ruin of a church in a ruin of a town high in the mountains, tells Billy Parham about it:

> We go from day to day, one day much like the next, and then on a certain day all unannounced we come upon a man or we see this man who is perhaps already known to us and is a man like all men but who makes a certain gesture of himself that is like the piling of one's goods upon an altar and in this gesture we recognize that which is buried in

18. *Blood Meridian*, 130.
19. *The Crossing*, 235-36.
20. *Cities of the Plain*, 285-86.

our hearts and is never truly lost to us nor ever can be. . . It is this for which we long and are afraid to seek and which alone can save us.[21]

The door opens when you see, unannounced, a man make a certain gesture. This gesture is "like the piling of one's goods upon an altar." We recognize in this gesture what has been buried, all along, in our hearts, though we've been afraid to seek it or perform it: the loss of everything we claim as our own. This gesture is, the ex-priest says, a "casual gesture" that accomplishes a "subtle movement of divestiture." It is not like the gesture made by the mute, mad and dramatic in its renunciation of words. But, despite its subtlety, the gesture nonetheless wreaks

> all unknown upon some ancillary soul a havoc such that the soul is forever changed, forever wrenched about in the road it was intended upon and set instead upon a road heretofore unknown to it. This new man will hardly know the hour of his turning nor the source of it. He will himself have done nothing that such great good befall him. Yet he will have the very thing, you see. Unsought for and undeserved. He will have in his possession that elusive freedom which men seek with such unending desperation.[22]

In this divestiture, a freedom attends the witness—that elusive freedom that men in desperation seek to enact through one or the other brands of nihilism. It comes suddenly, unannounced, unsought for, undeserved. It shows, McCarthy warns us, that "this life of yours is not a picture of the world. It is the world itself and it is composed not of bone or dream or time but of worship. Nothing else can contain it. Nothing else be by it contained."[23] This gesture of divestiture requires the witness to adopt a silence that is blind, that no longer claims to be able to picture the world, that burns its pictures of the world upon the world's altar. Then, in this blindness, something other than the picture of the world can show itself and you can see that even "this life of yours is not a picture of the world" but "the world itself."

Starving, Billy Parham is fed by a blind man who lost his eyes to war. The blind, he explains to Billy, have this advantage over those with eyes. Those with eyes still think that they can picture the world. And, more, they still think that such picturing is possible because "eyes

---

21. *The Crossing*, 153.
22. Ibid., 158.
23. *Cities of the Plain*, 287.

may select what they wish to see."[24] It is different for the blind. "For the blind the world appears of its own will. He said that for the blind everything was abruptly at hand, that nothing ever announced its approach. Origins and destinations became but rumors. To move is to abut against the world. Sit quietly and it vanishes."[25] Absent sight, distance and selection vanish. What's left is the pressure of the world that, busy picturing things, we hadn't noticed abutting against us. Sit quietly, sightless, and you'll recognize the sound of the world because, like the horses that stop grazing, it will disappear. "In his blindness," the blind man continues, "he had indeed lost himself and all memory of himself yet he had found in the deepest dark of that loss that there was also a ground and there one must begin."[26]

Having accomplished that subtle gesture of divestiture—or, better, having had that gesture wrought upon him—the blind man lost himself and all memory. He was enveloped in the deepest dark. But there, in that darkness, he sat down on the ground, quiet. And, sitting quietly, he discovered the ground he was sitting on. Grounded in this way, it became possible to begin again.

> The world has no name, he said. The names of the ceros and the sierras and the deserts exist only on maps. We name them that we do not lose our way. Yet it was because the way was lost to us already that we have made those names. The world cannot be lost. We are the ones. And it is because these names and these coordinates are our own naming that they cannot save us. That they cannot find for us the way again.[27]

The ex-priest of *The Crossing* shows Billy this same thing. He lives alone in the ruin of a church surrounded only by cats. But it turns out that, before being a priest, he was a Mormon. "I am a Mormon," he says of himself by way of introduction.

> Or I was. I was a Mormon born.
> [Billy] wasn't sure what a Mormon was. He looked at the room. He looked at the cats.
> They came here many years ago. Eighteen and ninety-six. From Utah. They came because of the statehood. In Utah. I was a Mormon.

---

24. *The Crossing*, 291.
25. Ibid.
26. Ibid., 291-92.
27. Ibid., 387.

Then I converted to the church. Then I became I dont know what. Then I became me.[28]

This is the sequence through which the gesture moves. The man was born a Mormon. It's just what he was. Then he named himself a Catholic and became a priest for a time. Then, one day, unannounced, he had wrought upon him that subtle act of divestiture and he abandoned meaning and burnt his picture of the world. He became, in effect, blind. And so he sat down on the ground. And he was silent. And, sitting, he found the ground of the world. And then, he says, "I became me." And so he began again.

"I was a Mormon. Then I converted to the church. Then I became I dont know what. Then I became me."[29] Such is the life of the witness.

---

28. Ibid., 140.
29. Ibid.

Bibliography

Agamben, Giorgio. *Nudities*. Translated by David Kishik and Stefan Pedatella. Stanford: Stanford University Press, 2010.

———. *The Time That Remains: A Commentary on the Letter to the Romans*. Translated by Patricia Dailey. Stanford: Stanford University Press, 2005.

Aurelius, Marcus. *Meditations*. Translated by Gregory Hays. New York: Modern Library, 2003.

Fink, Bruce. *A Clinical Introduction to Lacanian Psychoanalysis: Theory and Technique*. Cambridge: Harvard University Press, 1999.

———. *Fundamentals of Psychoanalytic Technique: A Lacanian Approach for Practitioners*. New York: W.W. Norton, 2007.

———. *The Lacanian Subject: Between Language and Jouissance*. Princeton: Princeton University Press, 1996.

Givens, Terryl. *Wrestling the Angel: The Foundations of Mormon Thought: Cosmos, God, Humanity*. New York: Oxford University Press, 2015.

Givens, Terryl and Fiona Givens. *The God Who Weeps: How Mormonism Makes Sense of Life*. Salt Lake City: Ensign Peak, 2012.

Harline, Craig. *Way Below the Angels: The Pretty Clearly Troubled But Not Even Close to Tragic Confessions of a Real Life Mormon Missionary*. Grand Rapids: William B. Eerdmans, 2014.

Latour, Bruno. *Reassembling the Social: An Introduction to Actor-Network Theory*. New York: Oxford University Press, 2005.

McCarthy, Cormac. *All the Pretty Horses*. New York: Vintage Books, 1993.

———. *Blood Meridian or The Evening Redness in the West*. New York: Modern Library, 1985.

———. *Cities of the Plain*. New York: Vintage Books, 1998.

———. *The Crossing*. New York: Vintage Books, 1995.

McConkie, Bruce. *Mormon Doctrine*. 2nd edition. Salt Lake City: Bookcraft, 1966.

———. "The Three Pillars of Eternity." *BYU Speeches*. Available at https://speeches.byu.edu/talks/bruce-r-mcconkie_three-pillars-eternity/

Melville, Herman. *Moby Dick*. New York: Modern Library, 1992.

Miller, Adam S. *Badiou, Marion and St Paul: Immanent Grace*. London: Continuum, 2008.

———. *Letters to a Young Mormon*. Provo, Utah: Maxwell Institute, 2013.

———. *Speculative Grace: Bruno Latour and Object-Oriented Theology*. New York: Fordham University Press, 2013.

Pound, Marcus. *Theology, Psychoanalysis, Trauma.* London: SCM Press, 2007.

Skousen, Royal, ed. *The Book of Mormon: The Earliest Text.* New Haven: Yale University Press, 2009.

Steinbeck, John. *East of Eden.* New York: Viking, 2003.

Uchtdorf, Dieter F. "The Gift of Grace." LDS General Conference. April 2015. Available at https://www.lds.org/general-conference/2015/04/the-gift-of-grace.

Index

Also available from
GREG KOFFORD BOOKS

Rube Goldberg Machines: Essays in Mormon Theology

Adam S. Miller

Paperback, ISBN: 978-1-58958-193-7

"Adam Miller is the most original and provocative Latter-day Saint theologian practicing today."

—Richard Bushman, author of *Joseph Smith: Rough Stone Rolling*

"As a stylist, Miller gives Nietzsche a run for his money. As a believer, Miller is as submissive as Augustine hearing a child's voice in the garden. Miller is a theologian of the ordinary, thinking about our ordinary beliefs in very non-ordinary ways while never insisting that the ordinary become extra-ordinary."

—James Faulconer, Richard L. Evans Chair of Religious Understanding, Brigham Young University

"Miller's language is both recognizably Mormon and startlingly original. . . . The whole is an essay worthy of the name, inviting the reader to try ideas, following the philosopher pilgrim's intellectual progress through tangled brambles and into broad fields, fruitful orchards, and perhaps a sacred grove or two."

—Kristine Haglund, editor of *Dialogue: A Journal of Mormon Thought*

"Miller's Rube Goldberg theology is nothing like anything done in the Mormon tradition before."

—Blake Ostler, author of the EXPLORING MORMON THOUGHT series

"The value of Miller's writings is in the modesty he both exhibits and projects onto the theological enterprise, even while showing its joyfully disruptive potential. Conventional Mormon minds may not resonate with every line of poetry and provocation—but Miller surely afflicts the comfortable, which is the theologian's highest end."

—Terryl Givens, author of *By the Hand of Mormon: The American Scripture that Launched a New World Religion*

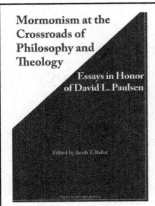

Mormonism at the Crossroads
of Philosophy and Theology:
Essays in Honor of David L. Paulsen

Edited by Jacob T. Baker

Paperback, ISBN: 978-1-58958-192-0

"There is no better measure of the growing importance of Mormon thought in contemporary religious debate than this volume of essays for David Paulsen. In a large part thanks to him, scholars from all over the map are discussing the questions Mormonism raises about the nature of God and the purpose of life. These essays let us in on a discussion in progress." —RICHARD LYMAN BUSHMAN, author of *Joseph Smith: Rough Stone Rolling*.

"This book makes it clear that there can be no real ecumenism without the riches of the Mormon mind. Professor Paulsen's impact on LDS thought is well known... . These original and insightful essays chart a new course for Christian intellectual life." —PETER A. HUFF, and author of *Vatican II* and *The Voice of Vatican II*

"This volume of smart, incisive essays advances the case for taking Mormonism seriously within the philosophy of religion–an accomplishment that all generations of Mormon thinkers should be proud of." —PATRICK Q. MASON, Howard W. Hunter Chair of Mormon Studies, Claremont Graduate University

"These essays accomplish a rare thing—bringing light rather than heat to an on-going conversation. And the array of substantial contributions from outstanding scholars and theologians within and outside Mormonism is itself a fitting tribute to a figure who has been at the forefront of bringing Mormonism into dialogue with larger traditions." —TERRYL L. GIVENS, author of *People of Paradox: A History of Mormon Culture*

"The emergence of a vibrant Mormon scholarship is nowhere more in evidence than in the excellent philosophical contributions of David Paulsen." —RICHARD J. MOUW, President, Fuller Theological Seminary, author of *Talking with Mormons: An Invitation to Evangelicals*

Re-reading Job: Understanding the Ancient World's Greatest Poem

Michael Austin

Paperback, ISBN: 978-1-58958-667-3
Hardcover, ISBN: 978-1-58958-668-0

Job is perhaps the most difficult to understand of all books in the Bible. While a cursory reading of the text seems to relay a simple story of a righteous man whose love for God was tested through life's most difficult of challenges and rewarded for his faith through those trials, a closer reading of Job presents something far more complex and challenging. The majority of the text is a work of poetry that authors and artists through the centuries have recognized as being one of--if not the--greatest poem of the ancient world.

In *Re-reading Job: Understanding the Ancient World's Greatest Poem*, author Michael Austin shows how most readers have largely misunderstood this important work of scripture and provides insights that enable us to re-read Job in a drastically new way. In doing so, he shows that the story of Job is far more than that simple story of faith, trials, and blessings that we have all come to know, but is instead a subversive and complex work of scripture meant to inspire readers to rethink all that they thought they knew about God.

Praise for *Re-reading Job*:

"In this remarkable book, Michael Austin employs his considerable skills as a commentator to shed light on the most challenging text in the entire Hebrew Bible. Without question, readers will gain a deeper appreciation for this extraordinary ancient work through Austin's learned analysis. Rereading Job signifies that Latter-day Saints are entering a new age of mature biblical scholarship. It is an exciting time, and a thrilling work." — David Bokovoy, author, *Authoring the Old Testament*

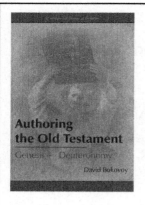

Authoring the Old Testament: Genesis–Deuteronomy

David Bokovoy

Paperback, ISBN: 978-1-58958-588-1
Hardcover, ISBN: 978-1-58958-675-8

For the last two centuries, biblical scholars have made discoveries and insights about the Old Testament that have greatly changed the way in which the authorship of these ancient scriptures has been understood. In the first of three volumes spanning the entire Hebrew Bible, David Bokovoy dives into the Pentateuch, showing how and why textual criticism has led biblical scholars today to understand the first five books of the Bible as an amalgamation of multiple texts into a single, though often complicated narrative; and he discusses what implications those have for Latter-day Saint understandings of the Bible and modern scripture.

Praise for *Authoring the Old Testament*:

"*Authoring the Old Testament* is a welcome introduction, from a faithful Latter-day Saint perspective, to the academic world of Higher Criticism of the Hebrew Bible. . . . [R]eaders will be positively served and firmly impressed by the many strengths of this book, coupled with Bokovoy's genuine dedication to learning by study and also by faith." — John W. Welch, editor, *BYU Studies Quarterly*

"Bokovoy provides a lucid, insightful lens through which disciple-students can study intelligently LDS scripture. This is first rate scholarship made accessible to a broad audience—nourishing to the heart and mind alike." — Fiona Givens, co-author, *The God Who Weeps: How Mormonism Makes Sense of Life*

"I repeat: this is one of the most important books on Mormon scripture to be published recently. . . . [*Authoring the Old Testament*] has the potential to radically expand understanding and appreciation for not only the Old Testament, but scripture in general. It's really that good. Read it. Share it with your friends. Discuss it." — David Tayman, The Improvement Era: A Mormon Blog

Common Ground—Different Opinions:
Latter-day Saints and Contemporary Issues

Edited by Justin F. White
and James E. Faulconer

Paperback, ISBN: 978-1-58958-573-7

There are many hotly debated issues about which many people disagree, and where common ground is hard to find. From evolution to environmentalism, war and peace to political partisanship, stem cell research to same-sex marriage, how we think about controversial issues affects how we interact as Latter-day Saints.

In this volume various Latter-day Saint authors address these and other issues from differing points of view. Though they differ on these tough questions, they have all found common ground in the gospel of Jesus Christ and the latter-day restoration. Their insights offer diverse points of view while demonstrating we can still love those with whom we disagree.

Praise for *Common Ground—Different Opinions*:

"[This book] provide models of faithful and diverse Latter-day Saints who remain united in the body of Christ. This collection clearly demonstrates that a variety of perspectives on a number of sensitive issues do in fact exist in the Church. . . . [T]he collection is successful in any case where it manages to give readers pause with regard to an issue they've been fond of debating, or convinces them to approach such conversations with greater charity and much more patience. It served as just such a reminder and encouragement to me, and for that reason above all, I recommend this book." — Blair Hodges, Maxwell Institute

War & Peace in Our Time:
Mormon Perspectives

Edited by Patrick Q. Mason, J. David Pulsipher, and Richard L. Bushman

Paperback, ISBN: 978-1-58958-099-2

"This provocative and thoughtful book is sure both to infuriate and to delight. . . . The essays demonstrate that exegesis of distinctly Latter-day Saint scriptures can yield a wealth of disputation, the equal of any rabbinical quarrel or Jesuitical casuistry. This volume provides a fitting springboard for robust and lively debates within the Mormon scholarly and lay community on how to think about the pressing issues of war and peace." - ROBERT S. WOOD, Dean Emeritus, Center for Naval Warfare Studies, Chester W. Nimitz Chair Emeritus, U.S. Naval War College

"This is an extraordinary collection of essays on a topic of extraordinary importance. . . .Whatever your current opinion on the topic, this book will challenge you to reflect more deeply and thoroughly on what it means to be a disciple of Christ, the Prince of Peace, in an era of massive military budgets, lethal technologies, and widespread war." - GRANT HARDY, Professor of History and Religious Studies, University of North Carolina, Asheville, Author, *Understanding the Book of Mormon: A Reader's Guide*

"Mormons take their morality seriously. They are also patriotic. Tragically, the second trait can undermine the first. When calls for war are on the horizon, it is possible for well-intended Saints to be too sure of our selective application of scripture to contemporary matters of life and death, too sure that we can overcome evil by force, that we can control the results of military conflict, that war is the only option for patriots. Yet pacifism has its own critics. This collection of differing views by thoughtful scholars comprises a debate. Reading it may save us in the future from enacting more harm than good in the name of God, country, or presumption." - PHILIP BARLOW, Arrington Chair of Mormon History and Culture, Utah State University, Author, *Mormons and the Bible: The Place of the Latter-day Saints in American Religion*

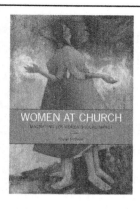

Women at Church: Magnifying LDS Women's Local Impact

Neylan McBaine

Paperback, ISBN: 978-1-58958-688-8

Women at Church is a practical and faithful guide to improving the way men and women work together at church. Looking at current administrative and cultural practices, the author explains why some women struggle with the gendered divisions of labor. She then examines ample real-life examples that are currently happening in local settings around the country that expand and reimagine gendered practices. Readers will understand how to evaluate possible pain points in current practices and propose solutions that continue to uphold all mandated church policies. Readers will be equipped with the tools they need to have respectful, empathetic and productive conversations about gendered practices in Church administration and culture.

Praise for *Women at Church*:

"Such a timely, faithful, and practical book! I suggest ordering this book in bulk to give to your bishopric, stake presidency, and all your local leadership to start a conversation on changing Church culture for women by letting our doctrine suggest creative local adaptations—Neylan McBaine shows the way!" — Valerie Hudson Cassler, author of *Women in Eternity, Women of Zion*

"A pivotal work replete with wisdom and insight. Neylan McBaine deftly outlines a workable programme for facilitating movement in the direction of the 'privileges and powers' promised the nascent Female Relief Society of Nauvoo." — Fiona Givens, co-author of *The God Who Weeps: How Mormonism Makes Sense of Life*

"In her timely and brilliant findings, Neylan McBaine issues a gracious invitation to rethink our assumptions about women's public Church service. Well researched, authentic, and respectful of the current Church administrative structure, McBaine shares exciting and practical ideas that address diverse needs and involve all members in the meaningful work of the Church." — Camille Fronk Olson, author of *Women of the Old Testament* and *Women of the New Testament*

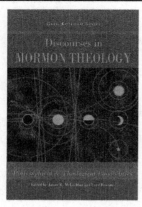

Discourses in Mormon Theology:
Philosophical and Theological Possibilities

Edited by
James M. McLachlan and Loyd Ericson

Hardcover, ISBN: 978-1-58958-103-6

A mere two hundred years old, Mormonism is still in its infancy compared to other theological disciplines (Judaism, Catholicism, Buddhism, etc.). This volume will introduce its reader to the rich blend of theological viewpoints that exist within Mormonism. The essays break new ground in Mormon studies by exploring the vast expanse of philosophical territory left largely untouched by traditional approaches to Mormon theology. It presents philosophical and theological essays by many of the finest minds associated with Mormonism in an organized and easy-to-understand manner and provides the reader with a window into the fascinating diversity amongst Mormon philosophers. Open-minded students of pure religion will appreciate this volume's thoughtful inquiries.

These essays were delivered at the first conference of the Society for Mormon Philosophy and Theology. Authors include Grant Underwood, Blake T. Ostler, Dennis Potter, Margaret Merrill Toscano, James E. Faulconer, and Robert L. Millet

Praise for *Discourses in Mormon Theology*:

"In short, *Discourses in Mormon Theology* is an excellent compilation of essays that are sure to feed both the mind and soul. It reminds all of us that beyond the white shirts and ties there exists a universe of theological and moral sensitivity that cries out for study and acclamation."
                    -Jeff Needle, Association for Mormon Letters

Exploring Mormon Thought Series

Blake T. Ostler

In volume one, *The Attributes of God*, Blake T. Ostler explores Christian and Mormon notions about God. ISBN: 978-1-58958-003-9

In volume two, *The Problems of Theism and the Love of God*, Blake Ostler explores issues related to soteriology, or the theory of salvation. ISBN: 978-1-58958-095-4

In volume three, *Of God and Gods*, Ostler analyzes and responds to the arguments of contemporary international theologians, reconstructs and interprets Joseph Smith's important King Follett Discourse and Sermon in the Grove, and argues persuasively for the Mormon doctrine of "robust deification." ISBN: 978-1-58958-107-4

Praise for the *Exploring Mormon Thought* series:

"These books are the most important works on Mormon theology ever written. There is nothing currently available that is even close to the rigor and sophistication of these volumes. B. H. Roberts and John A. Widtsoe may have had interesting insights in the early part of the twentieth century, but they had neither the temperament nor the training to give a rigorous defense of their views in dialogue with a wider stream of Christian theology. Sterling McMurrin and Truman Madsen had the capacity to engage Mormon theology at this level, but neither one did."

—Neal A. Maxwell Institute, Brigham Young University

Fire on the Horizon:
A Meditation on the Endowment and Love of Atonement

Blake T. Ostler

Paperback, ISBN: 978-1-58958-553-9

Blake Ostler, author of the groundbreaking Exploring Mormon Thought series, explores two of the most important and central aspects of Mormon theology and practice: the Atonement and the temple endowment. Utilizing observations from Søren Kierkegaard, Martin Buber, and others, Ostler offers further insights on what it means to become alienated from God and to once again have at-one-ment with Him.

Praise for *Fire on the Horizon*:

"*Fire on the Horizon* distills decades of reading, argument, and reflection into one potent dose. Urgent, sharp, and intimate, it's Ostler at his best." — Adam S. Miller, author of *Rube Goldberg Machines: Essays in Mormon Theology*

"Blake Ostler has been one of the most stimulating, deep, and original thinkers in the Latter-day Saint community. This book continues and consolidates that status. His work demonstrates that Mormonism can, and indeed does, offer profound nourishment for reflective minds and soul-satisfying insights for thoughtful believers." — Daniel C. Peterson, editor of *Interpreter: A Journal of Mormon Scripture*

Dead Wood and Rushing Water: Essays on Mormon Faith, Culture, and Family

Boyd Jay Petersen

Paperback, ISBN: 978-1-58958-658-1

For over a decade, Boyd Petersen has been an active voice in Mormon studies and thought. In essays that steer a course between apologetics and criticism, striving for the balance of what Eugene England once called the "radical middle," he explores various aspects of Mormon life and culture—from the Dream Mine near Salem, Utah, to the challenges that Latter-day Saints of the millennial generation face today.

Praise for *Dead Wood and Rushing Water*:

"*Dead Wood and Rushing Water* gives us a reflective, striving, wise soul ruminating on his world. In the tradition of Eugene England, Petersen examines everything in his Mormon life from the gold plates to missions to dream mines to doubt and on to Glenn Beck, Hugh Nibley, and gender. It is a book I had trouble putting down." — Richard L. Bushman, author of *Joseph Smith: Rough Stone Rolling*

"Boyd Petersen is correct when he says that Mormons have a deep hunger for personal stories—at least when they are as thoughtful and well-crafted as the ones he shares in this collection." — Jana Riess, author of *The Twible* and *Flunking Sainthood*

"Boyd Petersen invites us all to ponder anew the verities we hold, sharing in his humility, tentativeness, and cheerful confidence that our paths will converge in the end." — Terryl. L. Givens, author of *People of Paradox: A History of Mormon Culture*

For Zion:
A Mormon Theology of Hope

Joseph M. Spencer

Paperback, ISBN: 978-1-58958-568-3

What is hope? What is Zion? And what does it mean to hope for Zion? In this insightful book, Joseph Spencer explores these questions through the scriptures of two continents separated by nearly two millennia. In the first half, Spencer engages in a rich study of Paul's letter to the Roman to better understand how the apostle understood hope and what it means to have it. In the second half of the book, Spencer jumps to the early years of the Restoration and the various revelations on consecration to understand how Latter-day Saints are expected to strive for Zion. Between these halves is an interlude examining the hoped-for Zion that both thrived in the Book of Mormon and was hoped to be established again.

Praise for *For Zion*:

"Joseph Spencer is one of the most astute readers of sacred texts working in Mormon Studies. Blending theological savvy, historical grounding, and sensitive readings of scripture, he has produced an original and compelling case for consecration and the life of discipleship." — Terryl Givens, author, *Wrestling the Angel: The Foundations of Mormon Thought*

"*For Zion: A Mormon Theology of Hope* is more than a theological reflection. It also consists of able textual exegesis, historical contextualization, and philosophic exploration. Spencer's careful readings of Paul's focus on hope in Romans and on Joseph Smith's development of consecration in his early revelations, linking them as he does with the Book of Mormon, have provided an intriguing, intertextual avenue for understanding what true stewardship should be for us—now and in the future. As such he has set a new benchmark for solid, innovative Latter-day Saint scholarship that is at once provocative and challenging." — Eric D. Huntsman, author, *The Miracles of Jesus*

CPSIA information can be obtained at www.ICGtesting.com
Printed in the USA
BVOW06s1243090516

447340BV00019B/106/P